Mastering Agile: A comprehensive guide to agile software development

By

Jeffery M. Falgoust

Book Introduction

In the domain of programming advancement, change is the main consistent. The steadily developing scene of innovation and client requests requires flexibility as well as a total reexamining of how we approach the art of making programming. In this unique climate, Spry has arisen as the directing light, offering a progressive method for building programming that isn't only versatile to change but flourishes with it.

This presentation makes way for the book, acquainting the peruser with the Deft upheaval, its fundamental beliefs and standards, and what's in store in the impending sections of the extensive manual for Dexterous programming advancement.

What's in store in This Aide

"Mastering Agile: A comprehensive guide to Agile Software Development" is your sidekick on the way to dominating Spry. Whether you're an accomplished Lithe specialist or simply beginning your Spry excursion, this book is intended to outfit you with the information, abilities, and motivation you want. Over the accompanying sections, we will dive profoundly into different Coordinated philosophies, like Scrum, Kanban, and Outrageous Programming (XP). You'll find out about the fundamental jobs in Lithe, including the Item Proprietor, Scrum Expert, and the advancement group. We'll investigate the basic ancient rarities like Client Stories, Item Excesses, and Run Overabundances, and the functions that keep Dexterous undertakings on target.

As we venture together, you'll acquire bits of knowledge into how Spry standards are tried, underlining ideas like consistent coordination and conveyance, test-driven advancement, and the craft of refactoring. Scaling Light-footed for enormous undertakings and incorporating it flawlessly with DevOps will likewise be revealed. Challenges frequently arise with Light-footed reception, and we'll examine normal entanglements and procedures to defeat them. You'll find how to gauge achievement and draw motivation from true contextual investigations.

As we close, we'll look into the future of Spry, investigating arising patterns and advancing practices that guarantee to reshape the product improvement scene. Is it true that you are prepared to leave on this trip? Go along with us as we unwind the universe of Deft, a strategy that praises versatility, coordinated effort, and, most importantly, conveying extraordinary worth to your clients.

This presentation makes way for the book "Mastering Agile," framing the meaning of Dexterous in the cutting-edge programming improvement scene, the fundamental beliefs and rules that support it, and a brief look at what perusers can anticipate that in their process should dominate Light-footed.

Chapter 1: Introduction to Agile

In the high-speed and steadily advancing universe of programming advancement, the capacity to adjust, answer, and convey worth to clients effectively has become foremost. Customary, unbending undertaking the board procedures have frequently demonstrated deficient in fulfilling these needs. It is here that Spry's programming improvement arises as a signal of development and versatility, everlastingly changing the scene of how we make programming.

What is Agile?

Nimble is a way to deal with programming improvement and task the executives that focus on adaptability, cooperation, and client centricity. It underlines iterative advancement, flexibility, and the conveyance of practical programming to put it plainly, continuous augmentations.

Key attributes and standards of Nimble include:

1. People and Interactions: Agile values individuals and their communications over unbending cycles and devices. Powerful cooperation among colleagues is fundamental.

2. Working Programming: Coordinated puts a superior on conveying practical programming as the essential proportion of progress. It underlines unmistakable outcomes over broad documentation.

3. Client Collaboration: Active cooperation with clients and partners is empowered all through the improvement cycle. It's tied in with cooperating to comprehend and address client issues.

4. Answering Change: Coordinated invites evolving prerequisites, even late being development. It focuses on adaptability and the capacity to adjust to evolving conditions.

5. Iterative Turn of events: Light-footed projects are broken into little, reasonable cycles or runs, each commonly enduring half a month. These emphases consider regular criticism and changes.

6. Constant Improvement: Agile groups consistently think about their cycles and results to distinguish regions for development and make fundamental variations.

There are different Coordinated philosophies, including Scrum, Kanban, Lean, and Outrageous Programming (XP), each with its arrangement of practices and standards. Coordinated standards can be applied past programming improvement, to regions like task the board, and item advancement, and that's only the tip of the iceberg, making it a flexible methodology for overseeing change and conveying esteem in various spaces.

The Agile revolution

Not long ago, programming advancement was many times described by extended project plans, broad documentation, and unbending cycles that could prompt postponed discharges, skewed results, and frustrated improvement groups. The cascade model, a conventional methodology, had its benefits yet was not generally reasonable for the inexorably powerful innovation industry. Then came Light-footed, an extreme change in mentality. Brought into the world from the dissatisfactions of customary improvement techniques, Deft was something beyond a system; it was a change in perspective. It embraced the intrinsic capriciousness of programming projects and flourished in a climate where change was the main steady.

Nimble isn't simply a solitary, unbending technique; it's a bunch of standards, values, and practices that focus on client-coordinated effort, responsiveness to change, and the conveyance of utilitarian programming. At its centre, Coordinated is about individuals, correspondence, and the persistent quest for greatness.

The Agile Manifesto

In February 2001, a gathering of seventeen programming thought pioneers assembled at a ski resort in Utah, USA. What rose out of this gathering was the Deft Pronouncement, a brief statement that caught the substance of Nimble programming improvement. It denoted an essential crossroads throughout the entire existence of computer programming. The four vital upsides of the Light-footed Proclamation were:

1. People and corporations over cycles and instruments: Lithe perceived that product improvement was at last a human undertaking. The centre moved from inflexible cycles and instruments to individuals who construct and utilise the product.

2. Working programming over thorough documentation: Deft recognized the significance of documentation however underlined that practical programming was the essential proportion of progress. It comprehended that code expressed stronger than words.

3. Client coordinated effort over agreement discussion: Spry esteemed client cooperation as a way to accomplish a common vision. It was tied in with working with clients, not only for them.

4. Answering change over sticking to the script: Nimble embraced change as a characteristic piece of programming improvement. It recognized that plans would have to adjust as understanding extended and the market developed.

This proclamation established the groundwork for Dexterous Center standards and practices. It urged groups to embrace change, convey working programming oftentimes, and connect with clients effectively.

Principles of Agile

While the Coordinated Proclamation gave a bunch of values and characterized an outlook, Nimble's fundamental standards developed these ideas and gave down-to-earth direction. Deft's twelve standards, motivated by the Pronouncement, go about as a compass for Light-footed specialists:

1. Focus on consumer loyalty through right-on-time and constant conveyance of significant programming.

2. Welcome evolving necessities, even late in development. Deft cycles tackle change for the client's upper hand.

3. Convey working programming as often as possible, with an inclination for more limited timescales.

4. Team up day to day with clients and partners all through the task.

5. Construct projects around roused people. Give them the climate and backing they need, and trust them to take care of business.

6. Utilise eye-to-eye discussion as the most proficient and successful method for correspondence inside a group.

7. Working programming is the essential proportion of progress.

8. Keep a practical speed of work for engineers and different partners.

9. Make progress toward specialised greatness and a great plan.

10. Keep things basic — amplify how much work is not done.

11. Utilise self-coordinating groups to advance the best models, necessities, and plans.

12. Ponder at normal spans how to turn out to be more successful, then, at that point, tune and change conduct as needs be.

These standards offer an extensive manual for Dexterous turn of events, underlining the significance of successive conveyance, cooperation, and nonstop improvement.

Chapter 2: Agile methodologies

Nimble techniques are a bunch of adaptable and versatile ways to deal with programming improvement that focus on cooperation, client criticism, and gradual advancement. In a quickly impacting world, where programming necessities and economic situations can develop quickly, Dexterous strategies give a structure to successfully dealing with these vulnerabilities and conveying top-notch programming.

1. **Scrum**: The Structure for Joint Effort

Scrum is perhaps the most generally taken on a Light-footed system. It gives an organized structure to sorting out and overseeing complex programming improvement projects. In Scrum, work is coordinated into little, time-boxed emphases called "runs," normally enduring two to about a month. Each run brings about possibly shippable item increases. Scrum groups are self-coordinating and cross-utilitarian, consisting of jobs, for example, Item Proprietor, Scrum Expert, and Improvement Group. Everyday stand-up gatherings and incessant partner joint effort are key to Scrum's prosperity. The iterative and cooperative nature of Scrum permits groups to answer changing necessities and client criticism rapidly.

Key Standards and Ideas of Scrum:

1. Roles: Scrum characterises explicit jobs inside an improvement group:

•Item Proprietor: Answerable for dealing with the item overabundance, focusing on highlights, and addressing the client.

•Scrum Expert: Goes about as a facilitator, eliminating hindrances, and guaranteeing the group follows Scrum standards.

•Improvement Group: Cross-practical, self-putting together group liable for conveying augmentations of working programming.

2. Artefacts: Scrum acquaints key relics with work with advancement:

•Item Overabundance: A focused rundown of elements and client stories addressing client needs.

•Run Overabundance: A subset of the item excess chosen for a particular cycle.

•Increase: The possibly shippable item that outcomes from a run.

3. Sprints: Runs are fixed periods, commonly two to about a month, during which improvement happens. The objective is to convey a possibly shippable item increase toward each run's end.

4. Daily Scrum: An everyday stand-up gathering where colleagues share their advancement, examine hindrances, and plan for the day's worth of effort.

5. Sprint Survey: A gathering toward the finish of each run to exhibit the conveyed augmentation and accumulate criticism from partners.

6. Sprint Review: A reflection meeting held toward the finish of each run to examine what worked out in a good way, what could be improved, and to design changes for the following run.

Applying Scrum to Nimble Programming Advancement:

1. Roles and Obligations: Nimble groups recognize people to satisfy the jobs of Item Proprietor, Scrum Expert, and Advancement Group. These jobs guarantee clear liabilities and compelling joint effort.

2. Product Build-up Administration: Lithe groups keep an item overabundance, populated with highlights and client stories addressing client needs. The Item Proprietor focuses on these things.

3. Sprint Preparation: Toward the start of each run, Deft groups lead a run arranging meetings to choose things from the item build-up to chip away at during the run.

4. Daily Stand-Ups: Lithe groups hold day-to-day stand-up gatherings to talk about progress, hindrances, and plans for the afternoon. These short gatherings cultivate correspondence and keep the group adjusted.

5. Sprint Execution: Dexterous groups work on the run build-up things determined to convey a possibly shippable augmentation toward the run's end.

6. Sprint Survey and Review: Toward the finish of each run, Deft groups lead a run audit to exhibit the addition to partners and accumulate input. A run review follows to evaluate the group's exhibition and plan upgrades for the following run.

Advantages of Scrum in Nimble Programming Advancement:

•Coordinated effort: Scrum encourages cooperation through its characterised jobs and services, guaranteeing that colleagues and partners are adjusted and locked in.

•Versatility: The iterative idea of Scrum permits Nimble groups to adjust to changing necessities and needs without any problem.

•Client Centricity: The Item Proprietor addresses the client's advantages, guaranteeing that improvement endeavours are lined up with the client's needs.

•Straightforwardness: Scrum's characterised antiquities and functions upgrade straightforwardness by making work apparent and working with correspondence.

•Productivity: The run structure empowers a predictable, centred work musicality and advances the conveyance of possibly shippable augmentations.

Difficulties of Applying Scrum to Light-footed:

•Social Shift: Associations might have to go through a social shift to completely embrace Scrum's standards and practices, especially on the off chance that they are progressing from conventional improvement draws near.

•Asset Reliance: Scrum groups require gifted individuals who can satisfy their characterised jobs.

•Intricacy: Scrum's organised system might present some underlying intricacy, which may not be appropriate for tiny or clear activities.

Scrum is a broadly embraced Lithe philosophy known for its organised structure, cooperative methodology, and iterative turn of events. It gives an unmistakable design to group jobs, functions, and curios that work with productive programming improvement. While it might require a few changes and a social shift, the advantages of applying Scrum in Dexterous programming improvement are significant, especially concerning client centricity, versatility, and proficiency.

2. **Kanban**: Envisioning and Advancing Work process

Kanban is one more Coordinated technique zeroed in on overseeing work processes and improving cycles. Beginning from Lean assembling standards, Kanban stresses envisioning work utilising a Kanban board, which addresses the phases of an undertaking. Work things, addressed via cards or assignments, travel through these stages, making bottlenecks and failures quickly noticeable. Kanban's draw-based framework guarantees that work is pulled just when there is a limit, forestalling the over-burdening of groups. It is especially successful for groups managing a constant progression of work or backing undertakings. Kanban advances steady enhancements by making groups more responsive and productive.

Key Standards and Ideas of Kanban:

1. Visualizing Work: Kanban sheets are vital to the strategy. Work things, frequently addressed via cards or tacky notes, travel through a progression of sections on the board. These sections address various phases of the work process.

2. Work Underway (WIP) Cutoff points: Kanban sheets remember limits for the number of things that can be in every segment at the same time. This forestalls over-burdening and assists groups with zeroing in on finishing work before continuing toward new undertakings.

3. Pull Framework: Work is manoeuvred into the framework because of accessible limits. Colleagues select undertakings from the "To Do" segment when they have the data transmission to chip away at them.

4. Continuous Improvement: Kanban urges groups to review and adjust their cycles consistently. By following and breaking down work things, groups recognize bottlenecks and shortcomings for development.

5. Flow and Effectiveness: Kanban intends to improve the progression of work through the framework, guaranteeing that things move flawlessly starting with one phase and then onto the next. This improves proficiency and decreases lead times.

6. Customer Concentration: The strategy accentuates conveying worth to the client by focusing on work things in light of client needs.

Applying Kanban to Dexterous Programming Improvement:

1. Visualizing the Work Process: Nimble groups use Kanban sheets to imagine their product advancement process. This makes it more obvious the situation with work things and distinguishes bottlenecks.

2. Managing WIP: Kanban limits the quantity of work that can be in progress all the while. Nimble groups can utilise these cutoff points to forestall overcommitment and keep a reasonable speed.

3. Pull Framework for Errands: Lithe groups practise a drawing framework, where they select undertakings to work on in light of their ability. This forestalls over-burdening and advances the productive utilisation of assets.

4. Continuous Improvement: Dexterous groups lead ordinary reviews to investigate their Kanban interaction and make essential transformations. This iterative improvement is a sign of Light-footed techniques.

5. Customer-Driven Approach: Kanban guarantees that Light-footed groups center around conveying worth to the client by focusing on errands that line up with the client's necessities and needs.

Advantages of Kanban in Coordinated Programming Advancement:

•Effectiveness: Kanban assists Nimble groups with working all the more productively by envisioning and improving their work processes.

•Diminished Lead Times: By smoothing out the progression of work, Kanban lessens lead times, permitting groups to convey programming quicker.

•Straightforwardness: Kanban sheets improve straightforwardness, making work apparent and empowering groups to successfully oversee it.

•Client Arrangement: The client-driven approach guarantees that Lithe groups are ceaselessly lined up with client needs and can answer evolving prerequisites.

•Adaptability: Kanban can be applied to different Lithe techniques, making it versatile for various sorts of tasks.

Difficulties of Applying Kanban to Light-footed:

•Starting Above: Carrying out Kanban might present beginning above as groups conform to new cycles and instruments.

•Social Shift: Some colleagues might be impervious to change, especially assuming they are acquainted with various advancement rehearses.

•Reliance on Perception: Kanban depends intensely on visual portrayals of work, which may not suit all colleagues' inclinations.

Kanban is a strong Coordinated technique that supplements programming improvement by picturing work processes, overseeing work underway, and enhancing productivity. Nimble groups can use Kanban to improve straightforwardness, decrease lead times, and keep a client-driven approach. While there might be a few starting changes and a requirement for social moves, the advantages of applying Kanban in Dexterous programming improvement are extensive.

3. **Lean**: Diminishing Waste and Boosting Worth

Lean is a bunch of standards and practices zeroed in on expanding esteem and limiting waste. It isn't restricted to programming advancement however can be applied across different enterprises. Lean reasoning underlines distinguishing and wiping out exercises that don't contribute worth to the client. With regards to Spry procedures, Lean standards lead to additional productive cycles. Lean empowers a culture of persistent improvement, where groups mean to decrease squandering, abbreviate lead times, and convey more worth to clients. It adjusts well to Spry's accentuation on conveying working programming often and keeping a manageable speed.

Key Lean Standards and Ideas:

1. Value: In Lean, esteem is characterised as anything that the client will pay for. The lean system focuses on exercises that straightforwardly add to this client-characterised esteem.

2. Value Stream: A worth stream is a start-to-finish process expected to convey worth to the client. In programming advancement, it envelops movements of every kind from idea to conveyance.

3. Flow: Lean advances the smooth progression of work through the worth stream, wiping out bottlenecks and postponements. This guarantees that worth is conveyed proficiently.

4. Pull Framework: A force framework guarantees that work is finished in light of client interest. Work is pulled just when there is a limit, forestalling overproduction and abundance stock.

5. Kanban: Kanban is a visual device utilized in Shelters to oversee and control the progression of work. It includes imagining work things, restricting work underway (WIP), and ceaselessly working on the interaction.

6. Eliminating Waste: Lean distinguishes a few sorts of waste, like overproduction, pausing, and superfluous handling. The objective is to take out these inefficient exercises.

Applying Shelter Nimble Programming Improvement:

1. Prioritising Worth: Lean stresses focusing on highlights or undertakings that carry the most worth to the client. Light-footed groups can utilise Lean standards to zero in on conveying high-need includes first.

2. Reducing Waste: Lean practices are instrumental in recognizing and diminishing waste in programming improvement. This incorporates killing superfluous documentation, upgrading advancement processes, and smoothing out correspondence.

3. Kanban Sheets: Lithe groups can utilise Kanban sheets to picture the progression of work and cutoff WIP. This assists groups with dealing with their abilities and guarantees that work advances without a hitch.

4. Continuous Improvement: Lean energises the constant improvement of cycles. Dexterous groups can utilise normal reviews to distinguish regions for development and roll out gradual improvements.

5. Pull Framework: Deft philosophies like Scrum utilise a drawing framework for overseeing work. Groups focus on a specific measure of work in a run given their ability, keeping away from overcommitting and guaranteeing centre around the most important things.

Advantages of Incline in Lithe Programming Advancement:

• Productivity: Lean practices assist Nimble groups with working all the more effectively by decreasing inefficient exercises and advancing cycles.

• Client Centricity: Rest's emphasis on esteem guarantees that Lithe groups are lined up with client necessities and assumptions.

• Persistent Improvement: Lean urges Nimble groups to review and adjust their cycles, prompting progressing upgrades ceaselessly.

• Straightforwardness: Visual instruments like Kanban sheets upgrade straightforwardness by making work noticeable, permitting groups to oversee it.

• Adaptability: Lean practices and standards are versatile to various Light-footed procedures, making them flexible for different sorts of activities.

Difficulties of Applying Shelter Dexterous:

• Social Shift: The reception of Lean standards might require a social shift inside associations, especially if they are utilised with additional customary methodologies.

• Introductory Above: Executing Lean practices might present starting above as groups acclimate to new cycles and devices.

•Protection from Change: Some colleagues or partners might oppose change, especially assuming they are acquainted with existing cycles.

Lean is a significant expansion to Lithe philosophies, as it gives a structure to boosting esteem conveyance, diminishing waste, and upgrading processes. Lithe groups can use Lean standards to further develop effectiveness, upgrade client concentration, and embrace ceaseless improvement. Be that as it may, associations ought to be ready for likely social moves and starting changes while applying Shelter Dexterous programming improvement.

4. **Extreme Programming (XP)**: An Emphasis on Specialised Excellence

Outrageous Programming (XP) is a Dexterous system that puts areas of strength on design practices. XP groups hold back nothing specialised quality by following practices, for example, test-driven improvement (TDD), consistent combination, and match programming. Regular deliveries, short criticism cycles, and client association are vital to XP's prosperity. The strategy empowers close joint efforts among engineers and clients to guarantee the product meets the changing requirements of clients. XP likewise advances straightforwardness, empowering groups to zero in on conveying the most basic elements first while keeping up with the adaptability to adjust to developing prerequisites.

Key Standards and Practices of Outrageous Programming:

1. Test-Driven Improvement (TDD): TDD is a key practice in XP. It includes composing tests for a piece of code before composing the real code. This cycle guarantees that the code meets its useful necessities and stays testable all through advancement.

2. Continuous Incorporation (CI): CI advances the act of routinely coordinating code changes into a common store. This takes into consideration early identification of combination issues and keeps a stable codebase.

3. Pair Programming: XP groups frequently use pair programming, where two designers cooperate on a solitary PC. This approach cultivates information sharing, further develops code quality, and lessens the probability of blunders.

4. Small Deliveries: XP energises conveying little, gradual arrivals of the product. Successive deliveries empower early criticism from clients and partners, making it simpler to adjust to evolving prerequisites.

5. Customer Cooperation: XP underscores close joint effort with the client or item proprietor. Clients are effectively engaged with characterising prerequisites and can change them depending on the situation.

6. Simplicity: XP supports straightforwardness in plan and code. Groups expect to do the easiest thing that attempts to address the client's issues, keeping away from superfluous intricacy.

7. Refactoring: Refactoring is the act of rebuilding code to work on its interior quality without changing its outside conduct. XP groups routinely refactor to keep code spotless and viable.

8. Collective Code Proprietorship: All colleagues are liable for the quality and support of the codebase. There is no "proprietorship" of explicit parts; all things considered, everybody shares liability.

The XP Lifecycle:

XP follows a repeating improvement process with the accompanying stages:

1. Exploration: In this underlying stage, the group and client characterise the venture's extension and targets.

2. Planning: The group separates the venture into little, reasonable undertakings. Clients and engineers cooperate to focus on these undertakings.

3. Iteration: Improvement happens, in short, emphasises, generally enduring a little while. Every cycle brings about a possibly shippable addition of the product.

4. Productionizing: This stage includes preparing the product creation, including last testing, reconciliation, and streamlining.

5. Maintenance: After the organisation, the product enters the support stage, where it gets normal updates and improvements because of client criticism.

Advantages of XP:

• Excellent Code: XP's thorough designing practices, such as TDD and refactoring, add to the development of great code that is not difficult to keep up with and broaden.

• Consumer loyalty: The solid accentuation on client coordinated effort and little, successive deliveries guarantee that the product lines up with client necessities and assumptions.

• Versatility: XP's iterative methodology makes it exceptionally versatile to changing prerequisites and economic situations.

• Effectiveness: Match programming and aggregate code possession improve information sharing and efficiency, prompting more proficient turn of events.

• Risk Decrease: Regular testing, nonstop mix, and early client criticism help recognize and resolve issues early, lessening project chances.

Difficulties of XP:

• Social Shift: Taking on XP might require a social shift inside the association, as it challenges conventional improvement rehearses.

• Asset Reliance: XP requires gifted designers who know all about its works, making asset accessibility an expected test.

• Documentation: XP's emphasis on working code might prompt lighter documentation, which can be a worry in profoundly directed businesses.

Outrageous Programming (XP) is a Dexterous procedure that sets the bar for specialized greatness in programming advancement. A restrained methodology stresses rehearses like TDD, constant incorporation, and match programming to deliver top-notch code. With its client-driven approach and versatility to change, XP has demonstrated success in conveying worth to clients and answering advancing prerequisites. Notwithstanding, associations considering XP reception ought to be ready for a social shift and guarantee they have the vital assets and ranges of abilities to understand its advantages completely.

5. **Feature-Driven Improvement (FDD)**: A Model for Element Driven Development

Highlight Driven Advancement (FDD) is a Coordinated approach that is especially reasonable for huge, complex programming projects. FDD sorts out improvement around highlights, making it appropriate for projects with various functionalities and broad advancement groups. In FDD, highlights are characterised, planned, and assembled gradually. This approach gives clear permeability into the headway of individual highlights, making it more straightforward to oversee huge activities. FDD puts areas of strength for an on-space demonstration and configuration, guaranteeing that the product's engineering stays rational and effective as it develops.

Key Standards and Ideas of FDD:

1. Feature-Driven Approach: FDD revolves around highlights, which are discrete, client-esteemed capabilities or parts of the product. The improvement cycle spins around recognizing, planning, and carrying out these elements individually.

2. Domain Item Displaying: FDD puts a solid accentuation on space demonstrating, where the group makes a nitty gritty portrayal of the issue area. This model turns into the establishment for understanding and fostering the highlights.

3. Process of Five Stages: FDD partitions the advancement cycle into five particular stages:

• Foster a General Model

• Fabricate an Elements Rundown

• Plan by Element

• Configuration by Element

• Work by Component

4. Regular Investigations: FDD accentuates the significance of customary examinations and surveys, both for the area model and the codebase. This keeps up with excellent consistency in the product.

5. Individual Component Groups: FDD advocates the arrangement of little, cross-practical groups, each answerable for creating explicit highlights. This division of work advances effectiveness and specialisation.

The Five Periods of FDD:

1. Develop a General Model: In this stage, the group cooperatively fosters a significant level space model, giving a common perspective of the issue space. This model goes about as a source of perspective points all through the task.

2. Build a Highlights Rundown: The group recognizes and makes a rundown, all things considered, to be carried out. Each component is depicted with a short name, a definite portrayal, and a gauge of the time expected for its turn of events.

3. Plan by Component: Elements are focused on in light of business esteem and assessed exertion. The group allows highlights to explicit cycles and doles out them to the proper advancement groups.

4. Design by Component: Improvement groups work on the nitty gritty plan of the relegated highlights, taking into account UIs, data sets, and framework interfaces.

5. Build by Element: Groups execute the highlights in light of the plan determinations. This stage incorporates coding, testing, and coordinating the highlights into the general framework.

Advantages of FDD:

• Organized Approach: FDD's organized interaction, with the reasonable division into stages and element-based improvement, gives an efficient structure to huge tasks.

• Clear Correspondence: FDD advances clear correspondence through space demonstrating and ordinary examinations, guaranteeing that everybody in the group grasps the product's necessities and progress.

• Productive Groups: Little, cross-utilitarian groups can work proficiently on individual highlights, prompting centred improvement and quicker conveyance.

• Quality Affirmation: Normal examinations and audits assist with keeping up with great code and plans all through the venture.

• Adaptability: FDD is versatile and can be applied to undertakings of differing sizes, from limited scope advancements to enormous endeavour-level frameworks.

Difficulties of FDD:

• Introductory Above: The course of space demonstrating and making a thorough elements rundown can be presented starting above, which may not be reasonable for tiny tasks.

• Intricacy: FDD's organised methodology can be seen as perplexing, and it might require experienced project supervisors and designers to carry out.

• Asset Reliance: Powerful FDD requires an adequate number of talented assets to make space models, foster elements, and direct customary reviews.

Highlight Driven Improvement (FDD) is a thorough Coordinated philosophy that puts areas of strength for an organized, including driven advancement, space demonstrating, and proficient joint effort. It offers a coordinated system especially appropriate for enormous and complex programming projects. FDD's attention to space displaying and standard reviews keeps up with top-notch code, while its adaptability permits it to be adjusted for different task sizes and ventures. Notwithstanding, FDD's organised nature might present starting above and intricacy, which should be painstakingly overseen for effective execution.

6. **Dynamic Frameworks Advancement Strategy (DSDM)**: Focusing on the Business Need

Dynamic Frameworks Improvement Technique (DSDM) is a Nimble philosophy zeroed in on guaranteeing that product advancement lines up with the quick business need. DSDM gives an organized system to the whole undertaking lifecycle, from practicality to execution. It underscores coordinated effort, successive conveyance, and the significance of focusing on work in light of business esteem. DSDM empowers the dynamic contribution of end-clients all through the venture, guaranteeing that the eventual outcome meets true necessities. DSDM can be especially helpful for projects where fast conveyance is pivotal.

Precious Stone is a Deaf system that offers an adaptable and versatile way to deal with programming improvement. It's not quite so well known as a few other Dexterous systems like Scrum or Kanban, however, it has earned respect for its capacity to oblige different task sizes and intricacies. Created by Alistair Cockburn, Gem Deft strategies come in various flavours, each custom-fitted to various task qualities, making it a flexible methodology for programming improvement.

The Quintessence of Precious Stone Methodologies:

1. Adaptability: Precious stone procedures perceive that one size doesn't fit all in programming advancement. Ventures can differ extraordinarily in size, intricacy, and criticality. Precious stone adjusts to these varieties, permitting groups to pick the strategy that best suits their particular task.

2. People-Centric: Precious stone puts areas of strength on individuals engaged with the improvement interaction. It perceives that achievement is profoundly reliant upon the abilities, experience, and coordinated effort of colleagues. Precious stone strategies advance a culture of cooperation, trust, and successful correspondence.

3. Frequent Delivery: Like other Dexterous philosophies, Precious Stone advances the conveyance of working programming to regular cycles. This takes into consideration early approval of headway and makes it more straightforward to adjust to changing necessities or economic situations.

4. Reduced Complexity: Precious stone energises rearrangements in the project board and advancement processes. It tries to diminish pointless intricacy, zeroing in on the main parts of the venture and killing interruptions.

Kinds of Gem Methodologies:

One of the special parts of Gem is that it comes in numerous flavours, each custom-made to various task qualities:

1. Crystal Clear: This is the lightest and least difficult kind of Precious stone. It is reasonable for little groups to deal with clear undertakings. Clear underscores continuous conveyance, correspondence, and effortlessness.

2. Crystal Yellow: Precious stone Yellow is intended for bigger groups and ventures. It adds more characterised jobs and cycles to oblige the expanded intricacy of bigger

undertakings. It's appropriate for projects that are reasonably complicated yet not excessively basic.

3. Crystal Orange: Precious stone Orange is for projects that are portrayed by high criticality. It adds more design, documentation, and custom to the improvement cycle. It's most appropriate for projects with higher stakes, like those with administrative prerequisites.

4. Crystal Red: Gem Red is for huge-scope projects with complex necessities. It presents more cycles, devices, and practices to deal with the complexities of such tasks. It's generally expected utilized in crucial or venture-level programming advancement.

5. Other Precious stone Flavours: Past the super four flavours, Gem strategies can be modified further to oblige explicit venture prerequisites and attributes. This versatility permits associations to adjust their Light-footed approach.

Key Standards of Crystal:

- Successive Delivery: Gem stresses conveying working programming habitually, taking into consideration early input and flexibility.

- Individuals First: Precious Stone perceives that achievement is driven by the abilities and communications of individuals engaged with the task.

- Osmotic Communication: Precious stone advances a correspondence-rich climate where data streams uninhibitedly among colleagues.

- Security and Simplicity: Gem looks to work on processes and decrease superfluous intricacy while guaranteeing well-being and consistency being developed.

Advantages of Gem Methodologies:

- Adaptability: Gem's different flavours permit groups to pick the system that best suits their venture's size and intricacy.

- Accentuation on People: By putting individuals at the focal point of the improvement cycle, Gem procedures empower solid cooperation and a positive group dynamic.

- Early and Continuous Delivery: Like other Lithe approaches, Precious Stone advances early and regular conveyance of important programming, guaranteeing that the task stays lined up with changing necessities and economic situations.

Gem Deft systems are a versatile and individual-driven way to deal with programming advancement. Their adaptability in obliging different task sizes and intricacies makes them a significant decision for groups and associations looking for a Spry methodology customised to their particular requirements. Whether the undertaking is little or huge, straightforward or intricate, basic or less in this way, there's reasonably a Gem flavour that can give a structure to progress.

All in all, Lithe procedures offer a different arrangement of ways to deal with programming improvement, each custom-made to explicit requirements and inclinations. They share normal standards like flexibility, coordinated effort, and client centricity, while additionally integrating extraordinary practices and systems to address different venture situations. Picking the right Lithe philosophy relies upon the idea of the undertaking, group elements, and the particular necessities of the improvement exertion. No matter what the decision, Spry techniques give an establishment to making great programming while at the same time staying receptive to change and conveying worth to the client.

Chapter 3: Agile roles and responsibilities

Dexterous strategies have changed the scene of programming improvement and task the board by advancing adaptability, joint effort, and client centricity. Inside Coordinated structures like Scrum, Kanban, or Outrageous Programming (XP), explicit jobs and obligations are characterised to guarantee that activities run as expected and that groups stay zeroed in on conveying esteem. In this far-reaching guide, we'll investigate these Coordinated jobs and their related liabilities from top to bottom.

1. **Product Owner:**

The Item Proprietor is an essential job in Nimble philosophies, frequently liable for directing the improvement group and guaranteeing that the item lines up with the client's necessities and business goals. Their essential obligations include:

- Characterizing and Focusing on the Item Backlog: The Item Proprietor keeps a rundown of highlights, client stories, and necessities known as the item build-up. This includes gathering input from partners, understanding client needs, and focusing on building things given their significance.

- Addressing the Customer: The Item Proprietor goes about as the voice of the client inside the advancement group. They are answerable for guaranteeing that the cooperation meets client assumptions and conveys esteem.

- Tolerating or Dismissing Work: When advancement assignments are finished, the Item Proprietor surveys the result and concludes whether it meets the acknowledgment standards and can be thought of as "done."

- Adjusting to Changing Requirements: Spry activities frequently include advancing necessities. The Item Proprietor should be adaptable and ready to adjust the item overabundance as the client needs change.

- Giving Clarity: The Item Proprietor explains prerequisites, addresses group questions, and gives the vital data to the improvement group to go with informed choices.

- Making a Common Vision: The Item Proprietor guarantees that the group has a common vision of the item's objectives and targets.

2. Scrum Master:

The Scrum Expert is a worker chief who assumes a vital part in working with and guaranteeing the smooth activity of the Scrum structure. Their essential obligations include:

- Working with Scrum Events: The Scrum Expert puts together and drives Scrum occasions, for example, run arranging, everyday stand-ups, run audits, and run reviews.

- Eliminating Obstacles: Scrum Bosses work to eliminate hindrances that block the group's advancement. This might include resolving outside issues, settling clashes, or assisting the group with defeating difficulties.

- Training and Mentoring: Scrum Experts mentor the advancement group and help them comprehend and follow Light-footed standards and practices. They likewise tutor the group in self-association.

- Guaranteeing the Group Sticks to Scrum: The Scrum Expert guarantees that the Scrum system is executed accurately and that the group follows Scrum standards and practices.

- Working with Consistent Improvement: Scrum Bosses lead the group in directing reviews to distinguish regions for development and work with the group to make essential changes.

- Safeguarding the Team: Scrum Bosses safeguard the group from outside interruptions and tensions, permitting them to zero in on their work during the run.

3. **Development Team:**

The Improvement Group is a self-putting, cross-practical gathering liable for conveying the item increase. In Dexterous systems, colleagues frequently satisfy a few jobs, like experts, originators, engineers, and analyzers. Their essential obligations include:

- Creating Gradual Features: The Improvement Group chips away at conveying steady item includes during runs, guaranteeing they meet the Meaning of Done.

- Teaming up in the Run Backlog: The group cooperatively chooses how to satisfy the things from the run accumulation and self-sorts out to successfully convey the work.

- Responsibility for Quality: The Advancement Group is responsible for the nature of the work they produce. This incorporates code quality, testing, and guaranteeing that the item meets the characterised acknowledgment measures.

- Adjusting to Change: Dexterous advancement groups embrace change and are ready to adjust to developing prerequisites all through the task.

- Transparency: Colleagues impart straightforwardly and straightforwardly with one another and the Scrum Expert and Item Proprietor to guarantee everybody is in total agreement in regards to the run's advancement and any issues that emerge.

- Everyday Stand-Ups: The Advancement Group takes part in day-to-day stand-up gatherings, sharing their advancement, difficulties, and plans.

4. **Stakeholders**:

Partners are people or gatherings outside the advancement group who have an interest in the task's result. Their essential obligations include:

- Giving Input: Partners give important contributions to the Item Proprietor to assist with moulding the item build-up and focus on highlights.

- Going to Run Reviews: Partners are urged to go to run audits to assess the conveyed increase and give criticism.

- Supporting the Team: Partners might be approached to help the improvement group by giving data or explanations during the venture.

- Adjusting to Changes: Coordinated projects frequently include evolving necessities. Partners ought to be ready to adjust to advancing task objectives and goals.

5. **Agile coach**:

In certain associations, a Deft Mentor is liable for directing groups and the association in their Dexterous reception. Their essential obligations include:

- Preparing and Education: Dexterous Mentors give preparing and instructive assets to groups and people on Nimble standards, philosophies, and best practices.

- Tutoring and Coaching: They offer direction and training to Scrum Bosses, Item Proprietors, and Advancement Groups, helping them comprehend and carry out Nimble standards successfully.

- Driving Nonstop Improvement: Spry Mentors work with groups and associations to recognize regions for development, empower a culture of learning, and work with change.

- Exhorting Leadership: Nimble Mentors work with hierarchical initiative to adjust Lithe reception to the association's objectives and values.

- Eliminating Impediments: They help groups and associations recognize and address obstructions that prevent their Deft reception and achievement.

6. **Team Lead**:

In a few Deft groups, there might be a leader or specialised lead liable for explicit specialized or space mastery. Their essential obligations include:

- Specialised Guidance: Group leads give specialised direction and ability to the improvement group, guaranteeing that building and specialised choices line up with project objectives.

- Organising Tasks: They might assist with planning assignments inside the group and guarantee that the cooperation lines up with the run's targets.

- Coaching Group Members: Group leads frequently tutor junior colleagues, sharing their insight and experience.

- Collaboration: Group leads work intimately with the Scrum Expert and Item Proprietor to guarantee that the group is on target to meet its run objectives.

All in all, Lithe jobs and obligations are fundamental for the fruitful execution of Coordinated procedures in programming advancement and undertaking the board. Every pretends an unmistakable part in working with correspondence, coordinated effort, and the conveyance of significant worth to the client. These jobs, when distinct and perceived, assist Deft groups and associations with embracing flexibility, straightforwardness, and client-centricity in their undertakings. While Scrum is perhaps the most generally perceived Coordinated structure, comparative jobs and obligations exist in other Lithe systems, like Kanban, Lean, and Outrageous Programming, acclimated to fit the novel necessities of each methodology.

Chapter 4: Agile Artefacts

Coordinated approaches have carried tremendous changes to the universe of programming advancement and undertaking the board. At the core of Deft are different curios, which incorporate archives, sheets, diagrams, and other unmistakable things that act as devices for improving correspondence, straightforwardness, and the conveyance of significant worth to the client. These Deft curios assume a critical part in Lithe cycles, guaranteeing that groups remain on track, work proficiently, and adjust to change. In this extensive aid, we'll investigate the vital Coordinated relics, their motivations, and how they add to Nimble achievement.

Prologue to Agile Artefacts:

Spry techniques, like Scrum, Kanban, and Outrageous Writing computer programs, are known for their emphasis on flexibility, joint effort, and client centricity. To help these standards, Light-footed groups use different antiquities that give design and permeability to the improvement cycle. These antiques assist groups with catching, imparting, and tracking data fundamental for project achievement.

1. **Product Backlog**:

The Item Build-up is a focal and dynamic curio in Lithe procedures, especially in Scrum. It fills in as a focused rundown of highlights, client stories, and prerequisites that characterise the work to be finished on a task. The Item Overabundance is overseen by the Item Proprietor and assumes an essential part in directing the improvement cycle.

Motivations behind the Item Backlog:

- Prioritisation: The Item Excess assists the group with grasping the overall significance of work things. Higher-need things are chipped away from the outset.

- Transparency: It gives straightforwardness into the item's necessities and future improvements, making it open to the whole group.

- Adaptability: The Item Excess is a unique curio, permitting the Item Proprietor to adjust to changing needs and necessities.

- Client Focus: It guarantees that the cooperation lines up with client needs, as the Item Excess addresses the highlights and client stories mentioned by clients or partners.

Making and Dealing with the Item Backlog:

Making an Item Build-up includes gathering input from partners, clients, and the group. This can incorporate thoughts, client stories, highlight demands, or any things that address work to be finished on the undertaking. These things are then coordinated, explained, and focused on by the Item Proprietor.

Key practices in making and dealing with the Item Build-up include:

- Client Story Writing: Everything in the Item Excess ought to be composed as a client story. A client story commonly follows the organisation: "As a [user], I need [feature] so that [benefit]."

- Estimation: The Item Proprietor might work with the improvement group to gauge the work expected for each overabundance thing. This guides in prioritization.

- Refinement: The Item Proprietor and improvement group intermittently audit and refine the Item Overabundance to guarantee that it is forward-thinking, all-around focused on, and clear.

- Build-up Grooming: This is the course of consistently returning to and refreshing the Item Excess. It recognizes new things, eliminates old ones, and guarantees that the top things are ready for impending runs.

2. **Sprint Backlog**:

The Run Overabundance is a Nimble relic that is well-defined for the Scrum system. It addresses the arrangement of client stories and undertakings chosen from the Item Build-up for a specific run. The Run Build-up is an impermanent responsibility however long the run would last.

Motivations behind the Run Backlog:

- Focus: It assists the advancement with joining centre around the particular work to be finished during the run, diminishing interruptions and changes.

- Transparency: The Run Excess gives straightforwardness into the turnout chosen for the ongoing run, making it open to the whole group.

- Commitment: It addresses the group's obligation to convey the things inside the run, giving an awareness of others' expectations and responsibility.

- Checking Progress: The Run Build-up is an instrument for observing advancement during the run, assisting the group with keeping focused.

Making and Dealing with the Run Backlog:

The Run Excess is made during the run arranging meeting, where the advancement group chooses the client stories and undertakings they accept they can finish in the impending run. The things from the Item Accumulation are moved to the Run Excess, and their acknowledgment rules are examined and explained.

Key practices in making and dealing with the Run Accumulation include:

- Estimation: The advancement group appraises the work expected for each errand in the Run Excess. This assists the group with grasping the extent of work for the run.

- Day-to-day Stand-Ups: During everyday stand-up gatherings, colleagues talk about their advancement on the things in the Run Accumulation, distinguishing any obstructions or difficulties.

- Adaptation: The Run Build-up isn't firmly established. Assuming that new data or changes emerge, the group can adjust by adding, eliminating, or altering things during the run.

- Meaning of Done: The Run Excess ought to characterise how it affects everything to be "done." This guarantees that the group has a common perspective of when a thing is finished.

3. **Increment**:

The Addition is the result of a run in Scrum. It addresses the possibly shippable item that is the aftereffect of the improvement work during the run. The Addition is a key Light-footed relic that shows unmistakable advancement to partners.

Reasons for the Increment:

- Convey Value: The Augmentation is a significant result that can be possibly conveyed to clients, showing the headway made by the group.

- Validation: Partners can survey and approve the Addition, giving criticism to the group during the run audit.

- Client Feedback: Augmentation is a substantial curio that can be utilised to assemble input and experiences from clients, assisting the group with grasping their necessities better.

- Transparency: The Augmentation addresses the work finished during the run, giving straightforwardness into the group's endeavours and accomplishments.

Making and Dealing with the Increment:

The advancement group is answerable for making the Addition during the run. The Addition incorporates everything that the group has finished, guaranteeing that it meets the Meaning of Done. The Meaning of Done is a bunch of rules that should be fulfilled for a thing to be viewed as complete.

Key practices in making and dealing with the Addition include:

- Quality Assurance: The Augmentation should fulfil quality guidelines to be thought of as possibly shippable. This incorporates testing, documentation, and some other prerequisites.

- Client Review: The Augmentation is surveyed during the run audit meeting, where partners give criticism and approve its fulfilment.

- Adaptation: In light of criticism and any essential changes, the group might make acclimations to the Augmentation to more likely line up with client needs.

- Transparency: The Augmentation ought to be noticeable to all colleagues and partners, giving lucidity about the headway made during the run.

4. **Kanban Board**:

The Kanban Board is a visual portrayal of the work process in Kanban, a Spry procedure that spotlights nonstop stream and proficiency. Kanban sheets use sections to address various phases of work, and cards to address work things. This Light-footed antique assists groups with following the situation with assignments and streamlining the work process.

Reasons for the Kanban Board:

- Envision Workflow: The Kanban board gives a reasonable representation of the work process, permitting the group to see the situation with work things initially.

- Work Underway (WIP) Limits: By setting WIP limits for segments, the Kanban board assists in controlling how much work is advancing, forestalling over-burdening and bottlenecks.

- Distinguish and Determine Blockages: The Kanban board makes it simple to recognize undertakings that are stuck or deferred, empowering the group to address and determine blockages.

- Transparency: The Kanban board upgrades straightforwardness by making work apparent, permitting colleagues to figure out the condition of continuous errands.

Making and Dealing with the Kanban Board:

Making a Kanban board is a clear interaction, frequently including an actual board with tacky notes or a computerised device. The board commonly has sections that address various phases of work, for example, "To Do," "Underway," and "Done." Cards or tacky notes are utilised to address work things.

Key practices in making and dealing with the Kanban board include:

- Setting WIP Limits: Characterise WIP limits for every section to control how much work is underway. This guarantees that the group keeps a consistent stream.

- Picturing Workflow:The board ought to address the work process and phases of work, giving a visual manual for the group.

- Constant Monitoring:Colleagues consistently update the board by moving cards as errands progress, guaranteeing that it precisely mirrors the condition of work.

- Customary Stand-Up Meetings: Everyday stand-up gatherings might be utilised to talk about the situation with assignments on the Kanban board and distinguish any obstacles.

5. **Burn down Chart:**

A Torch Outline is a visual portrayal of outstanding work over the long haul in Deft philosophies, especially in Scrum. It assists the group with the following advancement inside a run by showing how much work is left to finish. Torch Outlines are a significant Nimble curio for project observing.

Motivations behind the Torch Chart:

- Progress Tracking: The Torch Outline assists the group and partners with following the group's advancement during the run.

- Predictability: It gives an understanding of whether the group is probably going to finish all the arranged work inside the run period.

- Early Detection: Torch Diagrams can uncover assuming that the group is falling behind from the get-go in the run, considering acclimations to be made.

- Focus: The graph assists the group with keeping fixed on run objectives and finishing arranged work.

Making and Dealing with the Torch Chart:

Making a Torch Diagram is a direct cycle. It regularly includes a chart with time on the x-hub and the leftover work on the y-pivot. The group refreshes the graph every day to mirror the headway made during the run.

Key practices in making and dealing with the Torch Graph include:

- Everyday Updates: The group refreshes the outline day to day, decreasing how much leftover work as undertakings are finished.

- Predictable Information Entry: Guarantee that information is reliably and precisely entered to keep up with the diagram's exactness.

- Pattern Analysis: The group can break down the outline's patterns to make forecasts about whether they will finish all arranged work inside the run.

- Noteworthy Data: The Torch Graph ought to give significant information, assisting the group with recognizing any fundamental changes or changes to remain focused.

6. **Burn-up Chart**:

A Consume Diagram is one more visual portrayal of work progress in Deft strategies. Following the finish of work things over the long haul, showing both finished and added work is utilized. Consume Graphs give a more extensive perspective on project progress contrasted with Torch Diagrams.

Motivations behind the Consume Chart:

-Progress and Scope: The Consume Diagram shows the advancement of work and how the task's degree might have changed after some time.

- Scope Change Management: It features when new work is added to the venture, permitting the group to successfully oversee changes in scope.

- Consummation Tracking: The outline gives an understanding of whether the group is on target to finish the arranged work within the given time.

- Partner Communication: Consume Diagrams are valuable for imparting project status and progress to partners.

Making and Dealing with the Consume Chart:

Making a Consume Diagram includes plotting the combined finished work and the total added work after some time. This gives an unmistakable perspective on how the venture's extension and progress change during the undertaking.

Key practices in making and dealing with the Consume Outline include:

- Information Accuracy: Guarantee that information is precisely recorded to give an exact portrayal of venture progress.

- Compelling Communication: Go through the Consume Outline to impart changes in degree and task progress to partners.

- Relative Analysis: Analyse the finished and neutralise the arranged work to decide whether the task is on target or the other hand assuming that degree changes are influencing progress.

- Run Limit Markers: Go through the Consume Graph to check run limits, making it simple to distinguish the headway inside each run.

7. **Definition of Done (DoD)**:

The Meaning of Done (DoD) is a basic Nimble curio that sets the standards for when a work is viewed as complete. The DoD gives a mutual perspective inside the group of what is generally anticipated from everything about quality and fulfillment.

Motivations behind the Meaning of Done:

- Quality Assurance: The DoD guarantees that work things meet a particular degree of value and culmination.

- Transparency: It gives straightforwardness by plainly illustrating the models that should be met for a thing to be thought of as "done."

- Lessening Ambiguity: The DoD decreases vagueness and guarantees that colleagues have a mutual perspective of what is generally anticipated.

- Client Satisfaction: An obvious DoD assists the group with conveying work things that meet client assumptions and requirements.

Making and Dealing with the Meaning of Done:

The Meaning of Done is cooperatively made by the group and ought to be factual and promptly available to all colleagues. The DoD ought to be inspected and refreshed depending on the situation to guarantee that it stays applicable.

Key practices in making and dealing with the Meaning of Done include:

- Collaboration: Include colleagues, including designers, analyzers, and different partners, in making the DoD guarantee a common perspective.

- Clarity: The DoD ought to be unambiguous, illustrating the particular models that should be met for a thing to be thought of as complete.

- Survey and Update: Consistently audit and update the DoD to adjust to changing task prerequisites and quality norms.

- Consistency: Guarantee that the DoD is reliably applied to all work things to keep up with the group's attention to quality.

8. **Retrospective action items**:

The Review Things to do are a bunch of explicit activities and enhancements that the group focuses on executing in light of the discoveries of the run review. These things are caught and followed to drive constant improvement.

Reasons for Review Activity Items:

- Nonstop Improvement: Review things to do to drive continuous upgrades to the group's cycles, joint effort, and execution.

- Criticism Loop: They act as an input circle, helping the group adjust and resolve issues raised during reviews.

-Accountability: Things to do make a feeling of responsibility inside the group to roll out and settle upon improvements.

- Transparency: By archiving and following things to do, the group keeps up with straightforwardness and guarantees that enhancements are tended to.

Making and Overseeing Review Activity Items:

Review things to do are made during the run review, where the group ponders what worked out positively, what could be improved, and what moves ought to be initiated. These things are then recorded and followed for finishing.

Key practices in making and overseeing Review Things to do include:

- Prioritisation: The group ought to focus on things to do because of their expected effect and plausibility.

- Ownership: Allocate proprietorship for each thing to guarantee that somebody is liable for its execution.

- Tracking: Keep a noticeable record of things to do and their status to guarantee they are finished.

- Follow-Up: During ensuing reviews, the group ought to audit the advancement of recently recognized things to do and survey their effect.

9. **Kanban Card**:

Kanban Cards are physical or advanced portrayals of work things in the Kanban philosophy. These cards are utilised on the Kanban board to follow the situation with undertakings as they progress through various phases of the work process.

Motivations behind Kanban Cards:

- Visual Tracking: Kanban cards give a visual portrayal of individual work things, making it simple to see their headway on the Kanban board.

- Restricting Work in Progress: The utilisation of Kanban cards upholds work underway (WIP) limits by showing the number of cards permitted in every section.

- Task Details: Kanban cards commonly incorporate insights concerning the errand, like its title, portrayal, and any significant data.

- Communication: The cards act as a specialised instrument, permitting colleagues to grasp the status and subtleties of each undertaking.

Making and Overseeing Kanban Cards:

Kanban cards can be physical, like sticky notes on an actual board, or computerised portrayals in a Kanban device. Each card ought to incorporate fundamental data about the work thing, like its title, depiction, and any related metadata.

Key practices in making and overseeing Kanban cards include:

- Clear Information: Guarantee that each Kanban card gives clear and pertinent data about the related assignment.

- Visualisation: Use tones or marks on the cards to give extra settings or data.

- Kanban Board Alignment: Ensure that the cards line up with the segments on the Kanban board to address the work process precisely.

- Consistency: Keep up with consistency in how cards are utilised and shown to guarantee a mutual perspective inside the group.

10. **User Story:**

A Client Story is a broadly utilised Light-footed relic that addresses a solitary unit of work or a utilitarian necessity according to the client's viewpoint. Client stories are in many cases utilised in Dexterous philosophies like Scrum to characterise client necessities and prerequisites.

Reasons for Client Stories:

- Client Focus: Client stories underline the client's requirements and give a reasonable comprehension of the normal usefulness.

- Prioritisation: Client stories are ordinarily focused on in light of client needs and worth, guaranteeing that the most important things are tended to first.

- Flexibility: Client stories are an adaptable configuration that considers changes and variations to client prerequisites.

- Communication: Client stories act as a specialised instrument between the item proprietor, improvement group, and partners.

Making and Overseeing Client Stories:

Client stories are ordinarily written in a particular organisation, for example, "As a [user], I need [feature] so that [benefit]." They are made by the item proprietor, and the advancement group and item proprietor cooperate to explain subtleties and acknowledgment rules.

Key practices in making and overseeing Client Stories include:

- Clarity: Client stories ought to be clear, succinct, and zeroed in on the client's point of view.

- Acknowledgement Criteria: Every client story ought to have related acknowledgment measures that characterise when it is viewed as complete.

- Prioritisation: Client stories ought to be focused on given client needs and business esteem.

- Story Points: A few groups use story focuses for assessment, permitting them to check the work expected for every client story.

- Input and Adaptation: Client stories ought to be routinely assessed and adjusted in light of client criticism and evolving prerequisites.

All in all, deft ancient rarities are apparatuses that empower groups to sort out their work, impart actually, and keep up with straightforwardness all through the product advancement process. These curios develop and adjust as the venture advances, assisting groups with conveying steady worth to the client in an adaptable and responsive way.

Chapter 5: Agile Ceremonies

Nimble functions are a bunch of fundamental ceremonies and occasions in Spry undertaking the board. These services assist Spry groups with teaming up, conveying, and planning, advancing straightforwardness and versatility all through the undertaker's life cycle. In this 2000-word article, we'll investigate the vital Dexterous functions, their motivations, and how they add to the outcome of Nimble activities.

1. Sprint Planning

Run arranging is the primary service in Coordinated, ordinarily held toward the start of each run, which is a period-confined cycle Light-footed. The primary targets of run arranging are to characterise what work will be finished in the impending run and to decide how it will be achieved. This function ordinarily includes the Item Proprietor, Scrum Expert, and the advancement group.

During run arranging, the group surveys the focus on an overabundance of things and chooses which ones to remember for the run. They gauge the work expected for each undertaking and focus on finishing a particular measure of work inside the run. This function cultivates joint effort and arrangement among colleagues, guaranteeing everybody comprehends the run objectives and the work in question.

2. Daily Standup (Everyday Scrum)

The day-to-day Standup, otherwise called the Everyday Scrum, is a short, day-to-day gathering where colleagues meet up to examine their advancement, difficulties, and plans for the afternoon. This service advances straightforwardness, helps the group recognize and resolve issues rapidly, and guarantees that everybody is in total agreement.

The Everyday Standup follows a bunch of three inquiries: What did you do yesterday? What are you wanting to do today? Are there any obstructions or snags in your manner? By responding to these inquiries, colleagues stay informed about one another's work and can offer help or answers for any issues that emerge.

3. Sprint Review

Toward the finish of each run, the group leads a run survey to feature the work finished during the run. The Item Proprietor and partners are welcome to this service to survey the work and give input. The essential objective of the run survey is to guarantee that the group has conveyed important and possibly shippable item increases.

During the run audit, the group exhibits the finished highlights or client stories and accumulates criticism from the partners. This input is fundamental for refining the item accumulation and changing needs, cultivating constant improvement.

4. Sprint Retrospective

The Run Review is a basic Lithe service that happens after the run survey. This gathering furnishes the group with a chance to consider their exhibition during the run and recognize ways of getting to the next level. The review plans to address what worked out in a good way, what could be improved, and what moves can be made to upgrade the group's productivity and viability.

Colleagues transparently talk about their perceptions and criticism, and together, they settle on things to do for the following run. The review is a vital system for constant improvement in Coordinated groups.

5. Backlog Refinement (Grooming)

Overabundance refinement, otherwise called prepping, is a continuous function wherein the group cooperatively surveys, explains and refreshes the item accumulation. This guarantees that excess things are obvious, appropriately focused on, and prepared for run arranging.

The Item Proprietor, Scrum Expert, and the improvement group partake in build-up refinement meetings. They separate huge client stories into more modest, noteworthy errands, update gauges, and add new things as needed. Prepping guarantees that the group generally has an unmistakable and modern overabundance to work from, making run arranging more proficient.

6. Release Planning

Discharge arranging is a more elevated level Coordinated function that spotlights the item's, generally speaking, guide and achievements. It adjusts the group and partners on long-haul objectives and needs. Discharge arranging is normally led for a couple of runs or a more expanded period, contingent upon the undertaker's scale.

During discharge arranging, the group and Item Proprietor talk about the elements and client stories that will be important for impending deliveries. They think about conditions, timetables, and targets to make a significant level arrangement. Discharge arranging gives a reasonable vision to the group and assists partners with understanding when they can anticipate that particular highlights should be conveyed.

7. Sprint Review

The run survey is in many cases a bigger scope form of the run audit. It happens toward the finish of a delivery or after a bunch of runs. The objective is to introduce the work achieved during the delivery to a more extensive crowd, including partners and executives.

The group grandstands the item's new elements, upgrades, and any progressions made during the delivery. This function is a chance for partners to assess the item and give input that can impact the following arrangement of needs.

8. Big Room Planning

Enormous Room Arranging is a cooperative occasion where Nimble groups meet up for key preparation and coordination. This function is especially valuable for enormous scope Nimble tasks including numerous groups. During Large Room Arranging, groups adjust their work, conditions, and needs, guaranteeing that the whole undertaking is on target.

Groups make a common guide, recognize chances, and synchronise their endeavours. This advances an all-encompassing perspective on the task and upgrades correspondence among groups, assisting with staying away from clashes and postponements.

All in all, Spry services are the foundation of the executives, giving design and cadence to groups as they work on conveying esteem gradually. Every function fills a special need, from arranging and execution to reflection and improvement. These functions cultivate straightforwardness, cooperation, and versatility, guaranteeing that Coordinated groups can answer change and convey great items that address client issues. Effective Spry reception requires a profound comprehension of these services and a pledge to their standards, eventually prompting a more proficient and responsive venture on the board.

Chapter 6: Agile principles in action

Dexterous standards have changed how activities are overseen and associations work. These standards, established in cooperation, flexibility, and worth conveyance, have turned into a directing light for groups across different businesses. In this conversation, we'll investigate how these Deft standards are set in motion, changing activities and associations the same.

1. Customer Collaboration over contract negotiations

In the Spry world, client joint effort isn't simply a trendy expression; it's a principal practice. Nimble groups work intimately with clients, regarding them as accomplices as opposed to clients. Rather than unbending agreements, they take part in continuous discourse and embrace client criticism. This guideline sparkles in real life when groups include clients from the venture's beginning. Whether it's product advancement, promotion, or item planning, customary gatherings, and criticism meetings guarantee the outcome lines up with client assumptions.

2. Working software over comprehensive documentation

Coordinated champions that functioning programming is the best proportion of progress. Practically speaking, this implies zeroing in on conveying useful programming in little, gradual deliveries. While documentation is fundamental, Light-footed groups keep it succinct and zero in on basics. This approach is apparent when programming advancement groups focus on code that has capabilities and can be exhibited to partners. There's no need to focus on comprehensive documentation however about substantial, working arrangements.

3. Responding to Change Over Following a Plan

Coordinated standards recognize that change is a consistent, not an exemption. Coordinated groups don't avoid transformation; they embrace it. Day-to-day stand-up gatherings are a substantial sign of this guideline, where groups adjust their arrangements because of every day updates and evolving prerequisites. Nimble groups are adaptable and change their course on a case-by-case basis, which makes them profoundly receptive to developing business scenes.

4. Individuals and commerce over processes and tools

Dexterous focuses on individuals and their communications over unbending cycles and apparatuses. Practically speaking, this rule empowers open correspondence and cooperation. Colleagues frequently accumulate for eye-to-eye gatherings or use video conferencing to guarantee that everybody figures out their errands and targets. It's tied in with cultivating a steady group climate where people cooperate, as opposed to being bound by cycles or devices.

5. Customer Fulfilment Through Right Time and Constant Programming Delivery

Spry's emphasis on client esteem is rejuvenated through right-on-time and nonstop programming conveyance. This implies delivering working programming, in short, emphasises, permitting clients to utilise the item sooner and give significant criticism. Whether it's a versatile application, a showcasing effort, or another help, Coordinated guarantees that worth is conveyed steadily, not toward the finish of an extensive undertaking.

6. Working Arrangements Over Far-reaching Features

Dexterous advances convey the base practical item (MVP) or a base attractive element (MMF) first. By and by, this implies groups focus on building barely an adequate number of highlights to make the arrangement usable. Subsequently, clients get a working item quicker. Light-footed groups then emphasise and improve the arrangement given criticism. This rule urges a speedy chance to-showcase without hanging tight for a total arrangement of highlights.

7. Collaboration with Clients and Partners All through the Project

Dexterous standards call for consistent commitment with clients and partners. This is seen in different Deft practices, for example, run surveys, where groups feature their advancement and assemble criticism from clients and partners. By keeping the lines of correspondence open, Dexterous guarantees that the task stays lined up with changing requirements and market requests.

8. Sustainable Advancement Pace

The economic improvement pace is something beyond a rule; training keeps groups from overstretching themselves. Coordinated groups gauge and plan given their ability, guaranteeing they can convey reliably. Measurements like torch graphs and speed help groups screen and deal with their speed, guaranteeing it stays reasonable all through the task. This training keeps groups stimulated and useful.

9. Technical Greatness and Great Design

Coordinated standards put areas of strength for specialised greatness and a great plan. In real life, this converts into rehearses like persistent refactoring to further develop code quality and address specialised obligations. Ordinary code audits and mechanised testing are fundamental to guarantee the product keeps up with excellence as it advances. The emphasis is on building a strong starting point for future turns of events.

10. Simplicity

The Dexterous standard of effortlessness calls for direct arrangements. Groups are urged to keep away from intricacy and over-designing. Whether it's planning a UI, a showcasing effort, or a business cycle, Coordinated groups make progress toward straightforwardness and tastefulness, bringing about additional sensible and viable arrangements.

11. Self-Arranging Teams

Deft standards advance self-arranging groups that have the independence to settle on conclusions about how they work and accomplish their objectives. Practically speaking, colleagues team up to decide the best way to deal with undertakings, cultivating imagination and possession. This approach permits groups to adjust rapidly to changes and difficulties.

12. Regular Reflection and Adaptation

Deft supports customary reviews, where groups consider what's functioning admirably and what needs improvement. This criticism circle guarantees ceaseless learning and transformation, prompting the refinement of cycles. Coordinated groups won't hesitate to change their techniques assuming that it implies improved results.

13. Delivering Worth is A definitive Proportion of Progress

At last, the Light-footed rule of conveying esteem is the litmus test for every single Lithe practice. Measurements like consumer loyalty, client commitment, and business influence become a definitive proportion of progress. In real life, Lithe groups effectively try to convey esteem and consistently survey their exhibition against these measurements.

All in all, Coordinated standards in real life are something beyond a bunch of rules; they address a groundbreaking mentality that impacts how work is moved toward in different businesses and undertakings. By embracing these standards, groups, and associations can all the more likely adjust to change, further develop item quality, and meet the powerful requirements of their clients. Deft isn't simply a task the executives approach; a way of thinking underscores client joint effort, flexibility, and the determined quest for esteem, driving development and progress in the cutting-edge business world.

Chapter 7: Scaling Agile

Scaling Coordinated alludes to the act of expanding Lithe standards and strategies past individual groups to address the necessities of bigger associations. Here are the central issues:

Agile at scale:

Spry at scale, frequently alluded to as "Lithe at Scale," is the use of Light-footed standards and philosophies to huge associations and complex activities. It includes expanding Spry practices past individual groups to arrange crafts by numerous groups and adjusting them to the association's essential objectives. Here are key parts of Nimble at scale:

1. Large Groups or Different Teams: In Light-footed at scale, you're managing bigger groups or various Deft groups chipping away at interconnected ventures or items.

2. Coordination and Collaboration: Deft at scale underlines viable coordination and joint effort between groups. This could include cross-group arranging, ordinary gatherings, and shared goals to guarantee arrangement.

3. Common Deft Frameworks: Associations frequently embrace laid-out Nimble scaling systems like SAFe (Scaled Coordinated Structure), LeSS (Huge Scope Scrum), Nexus, or Father (Trained Light-footed Conveyance) to give an organised way to deal with scaling Spry.

4. Backlog Management: Dealing with a solitary item excess or planning various group overabundances is a typical test. Prioritisation and arrangement with hierarchical targets are basic.

5. Alignment with Hierarchical Goals: Light-footed at scale requires major areas of strength for the association's essential objectives, guaranteeing that Spry practices add to the general mission.

6. Leadership Support: Initiative assumes a vital part in empowering Lithe at scale. Pioneers need to advocate Dexterous standards, give assets, and eliminate obstacles.

7. Continuous Improvement: Standard reviews and input circles ought to be important for the interaction to recognize regions for development at both the group and authoritative levels.

8. Decentralised Choice Making: Groups are frequently engaged to go with choices connected with their work, advancing quicker critical thinking and versatility.

9. Transparency and Communication: Compelling correspondence and straightforwardness are fundamental for progress. This incorporates sharing data, progress, and obstacles across groups.

10. Scaling Devices and Technology: Associations might put resources into apparatuses and innovation that help Lithe at scale, assisting with coordinated effort, following advancement, and overseeing bigger responsibilities.

11. Cultural Shift: Coordinated at scale frequently requires a social shift towards greater adaptability, client centre, and an eagerness to try and learn.

Dexterous at scale is a difficult, however compensating, attempt, as it permits enormous associations to be more versatile, client-driven, and receptive to changing economic situations. The particular methodology can differ contingent on the association's exceptional requirements, industry, and culture.

Large-scale scrum (leSS):

Large Scrum (leSS) is a Lithe system that stretches out Scrum standards and practices to address the intricacies of huge associations. Here are a few critical elements and ideas of LeSS:

1. Scalable Scrum: LeSS is a Light-footed system for scaling Scrum. It expects to keep up with the centre effortlessness and standards of Scrum while extending them to work in enormous, multi-group conditions.

2. Single Scrum: In LeSS, there is just a single item excess and one Meaning of Accomplished for all groups dealing with a similar item. This advances mutual perspective and arrangement across groups.

3. Teams and Roles: LeSS comprises numerous Scrum groups, each with its Scrum Expert and Item Proprietor. There are no extra layers of executives or jobs past these center Scrum jobs.

4. Team Self-Organization: Each group is self-coordinating and cross-useful, liable for conveying possibly shippable item augments.

5. Integration and Coordination: Groups in LeSS direction and coordinate their work in Run Audits and Item Excess Refinement meetings. Getting group coordination is normally finished through delegates from each group.

6. Principles over Practices: LeSS stresses adherence to Deft standards over inflexible adherence to rehearses. Groups are urged to track down the most ideal way to apply Scrum inside their unique situation.

7. Sprint Planning: Huge Scope Scrum commonly has a solitary Run Arranging occasion where groups cooperatively plan and resolve to work for the impending Run.

8. Transparency: Straightforwardness is urgent in LeSS. Groups share data about their work, progress, and obstructions transparently, advancing permeability and early issue discovery.

9. Continuous Improvement: Like normal Scrum, LeSS incorporates Run Reviews for groups to assess and adjust their cycles.

10. Organisational Change: Executing LeSS frequently requires a social change in the association to line up with Lithe qualities and standards. Administration backing and responsibility are fundamental.

Less is intended to assist enormous associations in accomplishing the advantages of Nimble, like quicker conveyance, work quality, and expanded consumer loyalty. By zeroing in on effortlessness and adherence to Scrum standards, it gives a system that can be redone to fit the novel requirements of various associations.

Scaled Agile frameworks(SAFe):

The Scaled Deft Structure (SAFe) is a well-known Spry system intended to assist huge associations with carrying out Nimble and Lean practices at scale. It gives an organised way to deal with applying Nimble standards across the whole association. Here are the vital parts and ideas of SAFe:

1. Core Values: SAFe is based on four fundamental beliefs: Arrangement, Work In Quality, Straightforwardness, and Program Execution. These qualities support the system and guide direction.

2. Principles: SAFe incorporates ten core values that assist associations with simply deciding, adjusting groups, and improving constantly. These standards support Lean-Spry reasoning and practices.

3. Four Levels: SAFe is coordinated into four levels: Group, Program, Enormous Arrangement, and Portfolio. Each level plays its parts, services, and ancient rarities, guaranteeing arrangement and coordination.

4. Agile Delivery Trains (ARTs): Expressions are the core of SAFe, comprising numerous Lithe groups that convey esteem in a worthy stream. Every Craftsmanship

works on a decent timetable and conveys an item increase during each Program Addition (PI).

5. Roles: SAFe characterises explicit jobs, including Delivery Train Specialist (RTE), Item Proprietor, Scrum Expert, and Framework Draftsman, to guarantee clear liabilities at each level.

6. Cadence and Synchronisation: SAFe advances the utilisation of normal rhythms and synchronisation focuses to adjust work across groups and levels. The Program Augmentation (PI) is a period boxed arranging stretch.

7. Lean and Frameworks Thinking: SAFe accentuates Lean and Frameworks Thinking, empowering associations to recognize and wipe out bottlenecks and improve the worth stream.

8. Backlog Management: SAFe incorporates Portfolio, Program, and Group excesses to oversee work at various levels. These accumulations are associated with and add to the progression of significant worth.

9. Continuous Conveyance Pipeline: SAFe backers for the making of a Ceaseless Conveyance Pipeline to empower quick and solid conveyance of significant worth.

10. Inspect and Adapt: The Examine and Adjust (I&A) studio toward the finish of each Program Addition considers a reflection and change of the methodology, execution, and design.

SAFe is an extensive system that gives rules and designs to huge associations to carry out Nimble standards while permitting adaptability to adjust to their particular setting. It is broadly taken on in businesses like money, medical care, and assembling to further develop item conveyance and responsiveness to showcase changes.

Disciplined Agile Delivery (DAD):

Disciplined Light-footed Conveyance (Father) is a Spry and Lean structure that gives direction to the whole arrangement conveyance lifecycle, from project commencement and engineering to conveyance and creation support. Created by Scott W. Ambler and Imprint Lines, Father is intended to be adaptable and adjustable to fit the particular requirements of associations. Here are a few critical parts of Father:

1. Full Lifecycle Approach: Father incorporates the whole arrangement conveyance lifecycle, including commencement, development, testing, sending, and creation support. It goes past the advancement stage to address the whole worth stream.

2. Principles: Father is directed by a bunch of rules that assist associations with settling on successful choices all through the conveyance interaction. These standards depend on Nimble and Lean reasoning.

3. Roles: Father characterises a few jobs, including Group captain, Item Proprietor, Engineering Proprietor, and Partner. These jobs assist with explaining liabilities and work with a coordinated effort.

4. Lifecycles: Father upholds numerous lifecycles, including Spry and Lean, as well as a breed approach that consolidates components from different life cycles. This adaptability permits associations to fit the structure to their particular setting.

5. Inclusive Process: Father is a comprehensive system that coordinates different Dexterous and Lean practices, like Scrum, Kanban, and Outrageous Programming (XP). It permits associations to pick the practices that turn out best for their necessities.

6. Phases: Father isolates the arrangement conveyance process into four stages: Commencement, Development, Progress, and Retirement. These stages give an undeniable level of construction to the task and help in arranging and following advancement.

7. Disciplined DevOps: Father advances the combination of DevOps works, underscoring the significance of coordinated effort among improvement and activities groups for productive and solid conveyance.

8. Enterprise Awareness: Father is intended to be undertaking mindfulness, meaning it thinks about the association's unique circumstance and lines up with its objectives and techniques. It assists associations with tending to complex difficulties that might traverse numerous groups or offices.

9. Flexibility: Father is profoundly adaptable and permits associations to pick their approach to work. It perceives that one size doesn't fit all and gives direction on fitting the structure to address explicit issues.

Father is appropriate for associations that need an even-minded and adaptable way to deal with Nimble and Lean practices, particularly while managing perplexing or controlled conditions. It offers direction for tending to a great many difficulties all through the arrangement conveyance process while considering adaptability and variation to special hierarchical necessities.

Scaling Nimble is a mind-boggling venture that requests responsibility, persistence, and an eagerness to embrace change. When executed, it can engage associations to turn out to be more nimble, receptive to advertising changes, and better prepared to convey worth to their clients.

Chapter 8: Agile tools and technologies

Deft instruments and advancements are programming and arrangements intended to help Dexterous turn of events and venture the executives' processes. These devices assist groups with arranging, tracking, teaming up, and dealing with their work. Here are a few normal classifications of Lithe devices and innovations:

1. Project Management and tracking tools:

- Jira: A broadly involved device for following and overseeing Nimble tasks, especially in Scrum and Kanban philosophies.

- Trello: A visual undertaking the executive's instrument that utilises sheets, records, and cards to coordinate errands and ventures.

- Asana: A work board device that upholds Spry philosophies and helps groups put together and focus on work.

2. Collaboration and communication Tools:

- Slack: An informative stage that works with constant correspondence and cooperation among colleagues.

- Microsoft Teams: A cooperative work area that coordinates with other Microsoft Office applications.

- Zoom: Video conferencing and specialised device for distant Nimble groups.

3. Version Control and Code Management:

- Git and GitHub: Famous variant control framework and facilitating stage for programming improvement.

- Bitbucket: Gives Git and Irregular vaults to groups to oversee and team up on code.

- GitLab: An electronic stage for overseeing Git storehouses, and CI/CD pipelines, and that's just the beginning.

4. Continuous integration and continuous delivery (CI/CD):

- Jenkins: An open-source robotization server that supports fabricating, conveying, and mechanising programming projects.

- Travis CI: A cloud-based CI/Disc administration that coordinates with GitHub storehouses.

5. Agile reporting and analytics Tools:

- Tableau: An information perception device that can be utilised to make Spry task dashboards and reports.

- Power BI: Microsoft's business examination administration for making reports and imagining information.

6. Requirements and product Management:

- Aha!: An item in the executive's stage that characterises item technique and makes guides.

- ProductPlan:A device for visual item road mapping and focusing on highlights.

7. Test The executives and Automation:

- Selenium: An open-source apparatus for mechanising internet browsers for testing.

- TestRail: An experiment with the board instrument for putting together and following programming testing endeavours.

8. Agile Portfolio Management:

- Targetprocess: A visual venture portfolio of the executive's device that oversees work across numerous Dexterous groups.

- AgileCraft (presently part of Atlassian): A Dexterous portfolio of the executive's stage that incorporates Jira.

9. Kanban Boards:

-KanbanFlow: An instrument that gives Kanban sheets to imagine work and oversee the work process.

- Kanbanize: A high-level Kanban board arrangement with examination and computerization.

10. Documentation and Information Sharing:

- Confluence: A cooperative work area for making, sharing, and examining content inside groups.

The decision of Deaf instruments and advances relies upon the particular requirements of your group, the Light-footed technique you're utilising, and your association's inclinations. It's crucial to select instruments that upgrade your Dexterous cycles, encourage joint effort, and further develop permeability into your task's advancement.

Chapter 9: Agile and DevOps

Nimble and DevOps are two firmly related approaches in the realm of programming advancement, each with its standards and practices. Here is an outline of both:

1. Agile:

- Principles: Light-footed is an adaptable and iterative way to deal with programming improvement that stresses cooperation, client criticism, and gradual advancement. It depends on the Light-footed Pronouncement, which diagrams values and standards, like people and connections over cycles and instruments, and answering change over sticking to the script.

- Methodologies: Lithe envelopes different techniques like Scrum, Kanban, and XP (Outrageous Programming), each with its practices. Scrum, for instance, partitions work into time-boxed cycles called runs, while Kanban centres around picturing and overseeing work underway.

- Benefits: Spry permits groups to adjust to evolving necessities, convey working programming in more limited cycles, and keep a nearby arrangement with client needs.

2. DevOps:

- Principles: DevOps is a social and specialised approach that expects to separate storehouses among improvement and task groups. It centres around robotization, coordinated effort, and constant conveyance.

- Practices: Key practices in DevOps incorporate computerised testing, ceaseless coordination, persistent conveyance (CI/Disc), and foundation as code (IaC). These practices plan to lessen manual intercessions, further develop programming quality, and speed up the delivery interaction.

- Benefits: DevOps empowers quicker, more dependable programming conveyance. It upgrades cooperation among designers and IT activities, prompting further developed effectiveness and decreased margin time.

integration of agile and DevOps:

Deft and DevOps are frequently utilised together to make consistent programming improvement and sending processes. This incorporation, known as "DevOps-Deft" or

"Dexterous DevOps," adjusts the turn of events and activities cycles. It guarantees that the product is created in an iterative, client-centred way (Deft) and is constantly conveyed with computerization and quality affirmation (DevOps).

Benefits of DevOps in agile

Coordinating DevOps rehearses into Nimble improvement offers a few critical advantages:

1. Faster Delivery: DevOps rehearses, like ceaseless mix and persistent conveyance (CI/Album), empower quicker and more incessant arrivals of programming. This lines up with The objective of conveying working programming in short cycles.

2. Improved Collaboration: DevOps supports close coordinated effort among improvement and activities groups, encouraging better correspondence and shared liability. This lines up with Light-footed accentuation on people and cooperation.

3. Enhanced Quality: Computerization in DevOps guarantees predictable and mechanised testing, prompting further developed programming quality. Dexterous qualities working programming, and DevOps guarantees that it isn't just working but additionally solid.

4. Quick Input Loops: Both Dexterous and DevOps advance quick criticism. DevOps, with its computerised checking and cautioning, gives input on the presentation and unwavering quality of the product, permitting Nimble groups to instantly answer issues.

5. Increased Adaptability: Deft is tied in with answering change. DevOps gives the specialised foundation to making changes rapidly and securely, diminishing the gamble related to changes underway frameworks.

6. Efficient Asset Utilisation: DevOps rehearses, similar to the framework as code (IaC), empower proficient asset the board and adaptability. This lines up with Spry's emphasis on augmenting the work not done, i.e., wiping out superfluous assignments and enhancing assets.

7. Reduction in Manual Effort: Computerization in DevOps decreases manual and blunder-inclined assignments, opening up groups to zero in on more important work, which is per Deft's rule of conveying significant programming effectively.

8. Customer-Driven Approach: Dexterous puts serious areas of strength on addressing client needs. DevOps guarantees that products can be conveyed to clients rapidly and dependably, lining up with a Light-footed client-driven way of thinking.

9. Risk Reduction: DevOps rehearses, like computerised testing and steady updates, diminish the gamble of significant disappointments underway. This lines up with Deft's inclination for overseeing gambles steadily.

10. Continuous Improvement: Both Spry and DevOps embrace a culture of constant improvement. Lithe's reviews and DevOps' checking and criticism components add to continuous improvements in cycles and programming.

DevOps upgrades the Spry interaction by giving the specialised and social practices vital for quicker, more dependable programming conveyance. It supplements Spry's client concentration, flexibility, and obligation to convey working programming in short cycles, at last prompting a more proficient and client-cordial improvement process.

In outline, Coordinated centres around the improvement cycle, stressing adaptability and client joint effort, while DevOps focuses on computerising and streamlining the organisation interaction. Together, they advance a culture of cooperation, fast turn of events, and dependable programming conveyance in present-day programming improvement conditions.

Chapter 10: Challenges and pitfalls

Difficulties and entanglements can be tracked down in different parts of life, and they are critical to know about to explore through them. Here are a few normal difficulties and traps:

1. Procrastination: Putting off assignments and obligations can upset efficiency and self-awareness.

2. Lack of Planning: Neglecting to plan can prompt disorder and botched open doors.

3. Communication Issues: Unfortunate correspondence can bring about misconceptions, clashes, and breakdowns in connections.

4. Financial Mismanagement: Misusing funds can prompt obligation, stress, and restricted monetary security.

5. Overcommitment: Assuming such a large number of commitments can prompt burnout and a diminished nature of work.

6. Inadequate Time Management: Unfortunate use of time effectively can prompt missed cutoff times and ineffective utilisation of time.

7. Health Neglect: Disregarding physical and emotional well-being can prompt different medical problems and diminished personal satisfaction.

8. Bias and Prejudice: Maintaining one-sided viewpoints can prompt segregation and frustrate self-improvement and cultural advancement.

9. Fear of Failure; A feeling of dread toward disappointment can deaden direction and breaking point potential open doors for development.

10. Resistance to Change: Being impervious to change can block individual and expert turn of events.

11. Lack of Resilience: Powerlessness to quickly return from difficulties can upset progress.

12. Lack of Adaptability: In a quickly impacting world, versatility is fundamental; unbending nature can be a critical entanglement.

13. Inadequate Ability Development: Neglecting to gain new abilities can restrict vocation, open doors and self-awareness.

14. Impulsive Choice Making: Settling on hurried choices without smart thought can prompt lament.

15. Unrealistic Expectations: Defining impossible objectives can prompt disillusionment and disappointment.

16. Stress and Burnout: Overexertion and consistent pressure can prompt physical and mental burnout.

17. Negative Self-Talk: Participating in self-analysis can harm confidence and frustrate self-improvement.

18. Dependence on Substances: Substance misuse can prompt fixation and serious medical problems.

19. Environmental Neglect: Disregarding natural worries can add to biological issues and worldwide difficulties.

20. Unhealthy Relationships: Poisonous or harmful connections can inconveniently affect mental and profound prosperity.

Exploring these difficulties and staying away from traps frequently requires mindfulness, strength, and an eagerness to learn and adjust. It's fundamental to remember them and find proactive ways to address or stay away from them in different parts of life.

Common pitfalls in Agile adoption

Light-footed systems have acquired far and wide notoriety in the realm of programming advancement and then some, with commitments to further developed productivity, adaptability, and consumer loyalty. In any case, regardless of the likely advantages, Light-footed reception isn't without its traps. In this article, we will investigate a portion of the normal entanglements that associations experience while endeavouring to embrace Coordinated rehearsals.

1. Shallow Implementation

Perhaps the most predominant entanglement in Light-footed reception is a shallow execution of deaf systems. Numerous associations rush to take on Light-footed wording and ceremonies, for example, day-to-day stand-up gatherings and run arranging, without completely understanding the hidden standards of Coordinated. Deft isn't simply a bunch of cycles; it's a mentality and a way of thinking. It underlines client cooperation, answering change, and conveying esteem iteratively. Without a profound comprehension of these standards, Lithe can turn into a simple façade, prompting dissatisfaction and frustration.

2. Protection from Change

Protection from change is a characteristic human response, and it can represent a critical test in Light-footed reception. Individuals inside an association might be OK with their current cycles and jobs. Changing to Spry frequently requires a basic change in how groups work, impart, and decide. Obstruction from colleagues who are worried about this change can dial back or even wreck the reception cycle.

3. Deficient Preparation and Coaching

Effective Lithe reception requests a guarantee of consistent learning and improvement. Without legitimate preparation and training, groups might battle to get a handle on the complexities of Coordinated procedures. Insufficient help and direction can prompt misconceptions, misinterpretations, and ineffectual Spry practices. Putting resources into legitimate preparation and experienced mentors can be a basic figure in staying away from this entanglement.

4. Overemphasis on Processes

Dexterous is tied in with esteeming people and their connections over cycles and devices, as expressed in the Nimble Statement. Be that as it may, associations in some cases become excessively centred around carrying out unambiguous cycles, similar to Scrum or Kanban, without giving due thought to individuals who will execute these cycles. This interaction-driven approach can prompt an absence of adaptability and versatility, which are central to Dexterous standards.

5. Conventional Hierarchical Structures

Another normal entanglement is endeavouring to fit Deft into customary, various levelled hierarchical designs. Nimble is intended to enable self-arranging groups and smooth orders to work with speedy independent direction. At the point when associations attempt to shoehorn Spry practices into their current designs, they frequently experience rubbing, as Lithe requires a more decentralised way to deal with the executives.

6. Absence of Ceaseless Improvement

Ceaseless improvement is one of the foundations of Spry. Notwithstanding, a few associations neglect to make a culture that empowers ordinary reviews and criticism circles. Without a promise to gain from errors and making steady enhancements, the advantages of Light-footed can stay slippery.

7. Scaling Issues

Light-footed practices might function admirably in little groups or tasks, however, when associations endeavour to scale Dexterous across bigger and more perplexing drives, difficulties can emerge. Organising different Deft groups, keeping up with consistency in item improvement, and overseeing conditions become more multifaceted. Without a thoroughly examined procedure for scaling Dexterous, associations can confront troubles in adjusting their endeavours.

All in all, Deft reception can be a groundbreaking excursion for associations, yet it's not without its traps. Shallow execution, protection from change, deficient preparation and instruction, an overemphasis on processes, inflexible hierarchical designs, and an absence of obligation to consistent improvement are a portion of the normal difficulties that associations might experience. Perceiving these entanglements and tending to them proactively is fundamental for a fruitful Nimble change. To genuinely understand the advantages of Light-footed, associations should embrace its standards, empower a culture of joint effort and versatility, and stay focused on the excursion of persistent improvement. Only at that time can Lithe follow through on its commitment to expanded productivity, adaptability, and consumer loyalty.

Managing protection from change

Change is steady on the planet, and it's especially unavoidable in the domain of business and associations. Whether it's adjusting to new advances, moving business sector requests, or carrying out various work processes, change is an inescapable piece of development and advancement. Nonetheless, with change frequently comes opposition, as people and groups normally will more often than not stick to the natural and the agreeable. Managing protection from change is a basic expertise for pioneers and associations looking to explore the fierce waters of change effectively. In this exposition, we will investigate the idea of protection from change, its purposes for it, and procedures to oversee and beat it.

Grasping Protection from Change

Protection from change can be characterised as the hesitance or resistance to modifying the state of affairs inside an association. This opposition can appear in different ways, from aloof obstruction (disregarding the change) to dynamic obstruction (transparently contradicting it). It's fundamental to perceive that protection from change isn't an indication of hardheadedness or pessimism; it frequently rises out of certified concerns and fears.

1. Fear of the Unknown: Change presents vulnerability, and people will generally be awkward with the unexplored world. Representatives could fear what the change will mean for their jobs, professional stability, or workplace.

2. Loss of Control: When change is forced on people or groups without their feedback, they might feel a deficiency of command over their work and climate. This can prompt obstruction as they try to recapture a feeling of independence.

3. Lack of Understanding: If the reasoning behind a change isn't conveyed, workers might oppose it essentially because they don't grasp the purposes behind the change or its expected advantages.

4. Past Negative Experiences: If past changes in the association were inadequately overseen or had unfortunate results, representatives might be careful about new drives.

5. Comfort with the Status Quo: Individuals will more often than not become alright with laid-out schedules and cycles. The disturbance brought about by change can prompt opposition as people are reluctant to get out of their usual ranges of familiarity.

6. Cultural and Profound Attachments: Hierarchical culture and customs can be profoundly imbued. Changing these can be met with obstruction, particularly assuming representatives have close-to-home connections to the present status.

Dealing with Resistance to Change

Managing protection from change is a nuanced interaction that requires a mix of sympathy, correspondence, and key preparation. Here are procedures for effectively overseeing protection from change:

1. Effective Communication: Straightforward and open correspondence is vital in addressing protection from change. Pioneers ought to make sense of the explanations behind the change, its advantages, and how it lines up with the association's main goal and vision. At the point when representatives comprehend the "why" behind the change, they are bound to help it.

2. Involvement and Participation: Including representatives in the change cycle can relieve opposition. At the point when people feel they have something to do with moulding the change or can give input on how it's carried out, they are bound to

embrace it. This interest can incorporate criticism meetings, conceptualising, or shaping change groups.

3. Education and Training: At times, obstruction emerges from an absence of information or abilities expected to adjust to the change. Giving the important preparation and assets can engage representatives to embrace the new cycles or advancements.

4.Addressing Dread and Concerns: Pioneers ought to recognize and address the apprehensions and worries of workers. This could include one-on-one conversations or gathering gatherings to give a stage for representatives to communicate their concerns. Compassionate listening can go quite far in mitigating these worries.

5. Celebrate Little Wins: Separating the change into more modest, sensible advances and celebrating little wins en route can make everyone feel better and inspired. It assists workers with seeing the improvement and advantages of the change.

6. Provide Backing and Resources: Change can be testing, and representatives might require extra help during the progress. This help could incorporate guidance, mentorship, or assets to assist them with adjusting to the new climate.

7. Lead by Example: Pioneers ought to set a model by embracing the actual change. At the point when representatives see their chiefs effectively supporting and taking part in the change, it can motivate certainty and decrease obstruction.

8. Feedback Circles and Adaptability: Laying out input instruments and staying versatile is critical to effectively change the board. As the change advances, pioneers ought to ceaselessly accumulate input, make changes, and exhibit that the association is focused on guaranteeing the change's prosperity.

9. Clear Goals and Measurement: Characterise clear targets and key execution markers (KPIs) connected with the change. This takes into consideration estimating progress and showing representatives that the change is delivering substantial outcomes.

10. Time for Adjustment: Perceive that change takes time, and people might require a time of change. Be patient and permit workers the space to adjust at their speed.

11. Leverage Change Agents: Recognizing and enabling change specialists inside the association can be profoundly compelling. These people can assist with supporting the change and impact their companions decidedly.

12. Managing Obstruction: confront or Coexist?

Not all protection from change ought to be gone up against or annihilated. At times, it very well may be more useful to coincide with specific parts of obstruction. For example, productive analysis or elective perspectives can prompt better change drives. Fundamental to separate between opposition thwarts progress and obstruction that offers important experiences.

In conclusion, Managing protection from change is a basic expertise for pioneers and associations. Figuring out the idea of obstruction, its hidden causes, and the different ways it can show is urgent. By utilising methodologies, for example, compelling correspondence, inclusion and cooperation, schooling, and preparing and tending to fears and concerns, associations can effectively oversee protection from change. Change, when explored insightfully, can prompt development, advancement, and upgraded hierarchical viability. Not the shortfall of obstruction means fruitful change to the board yet rather the capacity to address it usefully and lead the association through change with strength and versatility.

Chapter 11: Measuring Agile Success

Dexterous strategies have turned into a staple in the realm of programming improvement and are progressively applied in different enterprises. The appeal of Spry lies in its commitment to further developed adaptability, quicker time-to-showcase, and higher consumer loyalty. Be that as it may, estimating the progress of Nimble reception can be a complicated errand. It goes past basic measurements like speed and torch outlines. In this article, we will investigate the subtleties of estimating Spry's achievement and the complex figures that come into play.

Key performance indicators (KPIs):

Key Execution Pointers (KPIs) are fundamental measurements utilised by associations to quantify their presentation and progress toward accomplishing explicit objectives and goals. KPIs give a method for following, assessing, and overseeing different parts of an association's tasks. They can differ fundamentally contingent upon the business, division, and explicit targets, however here are a few normal classes and instances of KPIs:

1. Monetary KPIs:

- Income Growth: Measures the expansion in income over a predefined period.

- Benefit Margin: Mirrors the productivity of an association by contrasting income with costs.

- Profit from Venture (ROI): Measures the profit from speculation for a specific task or drive.

- Cost per Securing (CPA): Tracks the expense of gaining another client.

- Cash Flow: Shows the liquidity and money position of the association.

2. Consumer loyalty and Devotion KPIs:

- Net Advertiser Score (NPS): Measures client devotion and eagerness to prescribe the organisation to other people.

- Consumer loyalty Score (CSAT): Assesses the fulfilment level of clients after collaborations.

- Client Beat Rate: Tracks the rate at which clients quit utilising an organisation's items or administrations.

- Client Lifetime Worth (CLV): Measures the drawn-out worth of a client to the association.

3. Functional Effectiveness KPIs:

- Stock Turnover: Measures how rapidly an organisation sells and replaces its stock.

- On-Time Delivery: Tracks the level of items or administrations followed through on time.

- Quality Imperfection Rate: Measures the pace of deformities or mistakes in items or administrations.

- Worker Productivity: Assesses the proficiency of the labour force in finishing responsibilities.

4. Worker Execution KPIs:

- Worker Satisfaction: Measures the happiness and confidence of the labour force.

- Worker Turnover Rate: Tracks the rate at which representatives leave the association.

- Execution Appraisals: Assesses worker execution through customary audits and evaluations.

- Preparing and Improvement Progress: Measures the advancement of workers in preparing and proficient advancement programs.

5. Deals and Promoting KPIs:

- Transformation Rate: Measures the level of potential clients who make an ideal move, like making a buy.

- Lead Age Cost: Assesses the expense of gaining new leads or likely clients.

- Deals Development Rate: Tracks the expansion in deals over a particular period.

- Showcasing Profit from Venture (ROI): Measures the viability of promoting efforts in creating income.

6. Task and Item Advancement KPIs:

- Project Consummation Time: Measures how rapidly projects are finished.

- Scope Creep: Assesses the degree to which project scope changes during its execution.

- Item Improvement Cycle Time: Tracks the time it takes to put up another item from an idea for sale to the public.

- Bugs and Defects: Measures the quantity of bugs or imperfections in programming or item advancement.

7. Site and Online Presence KPIs:

- Site Traffic: Tracks the quantity of guests to a site.

- Skip Rate: Measures the level of guests who explore away from the site after reviewing just a single page.

- Transformation Rate: Assesses the level of site guests who make an ideal move, for example, joining or making a buy.

- Active visitor clicking percentage (CTR): Measures the level of clients who click on a particular connection or promotion.

These are only a determination of KPIs, and the decision of KPIs ought to line up with an association's essential objectives and needs. It's vital to choose KPIs that are explicit, quantifiable, feasible, important, and time-bound (Savvy) to screen and further develop execution. Consistently following and investigating KPIs can give important experiences and drive information-informed dynamics inside an association.

Traditional metrics versus agile Metrics

Before jumping into estimating Spry's achievement, it's critical to comprehend the distinction between conventional venture executives' measurements and those utilised in Dexterous.

Customary measurements, frequently connected with Cascade project executives, underline exercises, for example, making complete venture plans, meeting foreordained achievements, and remaining inside the financial plan. The outcome in this setting is in many cases estimated by how much these predefined plans are executed. In any case, this approach can be restricted in a powerful climate where necessities and needs might change.

Interestingly, Lithe measurements are more centred around conveying worth to the client. Dexterous achievement is estimated by how well the group answers change, the nature of the conveyed item, and consumer loyalty. While conventional measurements focus on process consistency, Dexterous measurements accentuate results and cooperation.

Key Metrics for Measuring Agile Success

1. Velocity: Speed, a typical Lithe measurement, gauges the rate at which a group finishes client stories or errands inside a run. It gives the best guess of how much work a group can deal with in a given time. While speed is significant, it's anything but an independent mark of progress. Groups ought to plan to further develop speed after some time however not to the detriment of value or versatility.

2. Lead Time and Cycle Time: Lead time is the term from the beginning of an undertaking (like a client story) to its consummation, including all stages like examination, improvement, testing, and sending. Process duration is the time taken to finish the genuine work once it starts. These measurements help in understanding the effectiveness of the improvement cycle and recognizing bottlenecks.

3. Customer Satisfaction: Dexterous achievement ought to eventually be estimated by consumer loyalty. This can be measured through Net Advertiser Scores (NPS), client input, or client acknowledgment rates. A fruitful Nimble group ought to persistently look for input from clients and repeat because of that criticism.

4. Defect Rate: The quantity of deformities or issues in the item is a significant measurement. Lower imperfection rates show higher item quality. Nimble achievement is intently attached to conveying a great item, and that's what this measurement mirrors.

5. Burn-Up and Torch Charts: While these are conventional Lithe measurements, they hold esteem. Consume graphs show how much work has been finished, while torch diagrams track how much work remains. Both give permeability into the group's advancement and can help in adjusting to changes in degree or needs.

6. Employee Satisfaction: Coordinated standards put areas of strength in propelled and self-sorting out-groups. High representative fulfilment is a mark of Nimble achievement, as it mirrors a positive workplace and arrangement with Dexterous qualities.

7. Adaptability: Light-footed is tied in with answering change, so estimating the group's capacity to adjust is significant. It very well may be reflected in measurements like the number of degree changes in an undertaking, the time taken to turn in light of criticism, and the achievement pace of adjusting to unforeseen issues.

Challenges in measuring agile Success

Estimating Lithe achievement isn't without its difficulties:

1. Subjectivity: Numerous Dexterous measurements depend on emotional information, like consumer loyalty or camaraderie. These are affected by different factors and can be precisely measured.

2. Context Matters: What is viewed as effective in one Light-footed group or undertaking may not make a difference to another. Setting explicit achievement measures is fundamental.

3. Short-Term versus Long-Term: Nimble accentuates short cycles and incessant deliveries. Estimating achievement exclusively on momentary measurements may not represent long-haul esteem conveyance and manageability.

4. Outcome versus Output: Spry achievement ought to zero in on conveying significant results to clients, not simply creating a high volume of results. Measurements that underline results are more pertinent.

The Agile Mindset

Estimating Coordinated achievement eventually goes past numbers. It is tied in with taking on a Dexterous attitude. This mentality values adaptability, joint effort, and a tireless spotlight on conveying worth to the client. Achievement isn't exclusively about gathering predefined designs but about answering change, gaining from input, and ceaselessly getting to the next level.

All in all, estimating Light-footed achievement requires a comprehensive methodology that thinks about a blend of quantitative and subjective measurements. It's not just about following numbers like speed and imperfection rates, yet in addition about zeroing in on consumer loyalty, representative assurance, and the group's versatility. Lithe achievement is, at its centre, about conveying worth and embracing an outlook that values dexterity, responsiveness, and ceaseless improvement.

Chapter 12: Case Studies

The spry approach is much of the time represented through contextual analyses to feature its viability. The following are a couple of notable models:

1. Spotify: Spotify's nimble change is generally considered. They took on a "clan crew" model, which advances cross-utilitarian groups and independence. Their case shows the way that enormous associations can scale light-footed rehearsals.

2. Scrum at Salesforce: Salesforce is a notable CRM organisation that took on Scrum, a famous light-footed system. Their contextual analysis grandstands how spry standards can be applied in different enterprises.

3. Agile at GE: General Electric (GE) went through a spry change to further develop its product advancement processes. The contextual analysis features how spry can be adjusted for assembling and tech organisations.

4. Zappos Holacracy: Zappos, an internet-based shoe retailer, changed to a self-administration model known as Holacracy. This contextual analysis represents how deft standards can be applied to hierarchical construction and culture.

5. US Computerised Administration (USDS): The USDS, an administration organisation, utilises spry philosophies to work on advanced administrations for residents. This case shows the materialism of dexterity in the public area.

These contextual analyses offer experiences into how coordination can be modified for various associations and ventures, stressing adaptability and ceaseless improvement.

Real-world examples of agile implementation

1. Microsoft Windows: Microsoft involved lithe practices in the improvement of Windows 7. They took on a more iterative methodology, with more limited improvement cycles, ceaseless client criticism, and an emphasis on conveying steady enhancements. This approach assisted them with answering client needs more quickly and discharging a fruitful item.

2. Amazon: Amazon is known for its dexterous way of dealing with programming advancement. They utilise a two-pizza group model, where groups are sufficiently small to be taken care of by two pizzas. This encourages joint effort, speed, and development. Amazon's capacity to quickly deliver new elements and administrations is a demonstration of light-footed standards in real life.

3. Spotify: Spotify is much of the time referred to as a great representation of light-footed execution. They arrange their improvement groups into "crews," "clans," and "societies," empowering independence and development. This design has permitted them to persistently develop and give an easy-to-use music streaming stage.

4. Adobe Systems: Adobe changed to dexterous practices in the improvement of their Imaginative Cloud programming suite. By embracing Scrum and dexterous standards, they further developed joint effort, diminished improvement cycles, and upgraded the client experience.

5. The UK Government Advanced Service: The UK's administration's computerised administration embraced spry strategies to upgrade advanced public administrations. Their spry methodology centers around client needs, iterative turn of events, and the conveyance of advanced administrations that residents see as instinctive and significant.

These models exhibit how light-footed philosophies have been applied in various businesses and associations, prompting more effective turn of events, further developed consumer loyalty and faster transformation to evolving necessities.

Future of agile

The fate of spry philosophy is probably going to keep developing to meet the changing necessities of associations and the innovation scene. Here are a few patterns and expectations for the future of deft:

1. Agile Past Software: Spry standards are growing past programming improvement and IT. They are being taken on in different businesses, including advertising, medical services, and government, to further develop projects, the board and item advancement.

2. Agile at Scale: Scaling lithe to enormous associations will stay a concentration. Systems like SAFe (Scaled Dexterous Structure) and LeSS (Enormous Scope Scrum) are probably going to acquire an unmistakable quality as organisations try to carry out coordination across their whole association.

3. AI and Automation: Deft practices will incorporate more computerised reasoning and robotization. Groups will use computer-based intelligence for information examination, testing, and navigation, making coordinated processes more proficient.

4. Hybrid Approaches: Associations might take on crossover techniques that consolidate light-footed with another task the executive's ways to deal with address

explicit issues. For instance, consolidating components of DevOps for persistent joining and conveyance.

5. Remote and Dispersed Agile: Remote work and conveyed groups are turning out to be more normal. Nimble practices will keep on adjusting to help powerful cooperation and correspondence in this climate.

6. Customer-Centricity: A more grounded centre around client-driven lithe practices, for example, Plan Thinking, to guarantee that items and administrations are worked with a profound comprehension of client needs.

7. Agile for Sustainability: Dexterous might be applied to manageability and ecological drives, assisting associations with turning out to be more versatile and receptive to developing natural difficulties.

8. Blockchain and Agile: In enterprises like money and store network the board, blockchain innovation might be coordinated with lithe to make more straightforward and secure frameworks.

9. Agile Mindset: Accentuation on the coordinated outlook and social perspectives will keep on being vital, as associations perceive that nimbleness isn't simply a bunch of practices but a perspective and working.

10. Data-Driven Choice Making: Coordinated will progressively use information examination for navigation and ceaseless improvement, prompting more information-driven cycles.

The future of lithe is probably going to be set apart by its flexibility in different areas and the combination of arising innovations. As associations look to turn out to be more responsive and client-engaged, light-footed systems will assume an urgent part in their prosperity.

Evolving trends and practices

Light-footed rehearses are persistently developing to address the issues of current associations. Here are some developing patterns and practices inside the universe of lithe:

1. Agile at Scale: It is turning out to be more normal to Scale coordinated philosophies. Systems like Protected, LeSS, and Spotify's model are being taken on to empower enormous associations to apply nimble standards across various groups and offices.

2. Value Stream Mapping: Associations are zeroing in on esteem stream planning to distinguish bottlenecks and shortcomings in their cycles. This enhances the whole worth conveyance framework, not simply individual groups.

3. Remote Agile: With the ascent of remote work, lithe practices are adjusting to help disseminated groups. This incorporates apparatuses for virtual reviews, everyday stand-ups, and cooperative web-based sheets.

4. Design Thinking and Agile: The incorporation of configuration thinking into light-footed rehearsals is developing. This mix underlines compassion, client-focused plans, and iterative improvement to make more inventive and easy-to-understand items.

5. DevOps and Nonstop Delivery: DevOps rehearsals are converging with dexterity to make a culture of ceaseless conveyance. This pattern underlines computerization, joint effort, and quick, dependable deliveries.

6. Customer-Driven Agile: A solid spotlight on client input and commitment, utilising techniques like Plan Run and Lean Startup, is turning into a central part of spry practices.

7. AI and Agile: Lithe groups are consolidating man-made intelligence and AI for information-driven independent direction, prescient examination, and robotizing routine errands to improve proficiency.

8. Kanban and Stream-based Approaches: Kanban, which underscores imagining work and overseeing it as a stream, is acquiring ubiquity for its adaptability and capacity to oversee work in a nonstop way.

9. Agile Authority and Management: Spry standards are stretching out past advancement groups to initiatives and executives. Lithe initiative supports a more responsive, versatile, and worker administration approach.

10. Behaviour-Driven Improvement (BDD): BDD works on, stressing coordinated effort between designers, analyzers, and non-specialized partners, are turning out to be more basic to nimble turn of events.

11. Agile for Non-IT Functions: Light-footed philosophies are extending past IT into other business capabilities like advertising, HR, and money, with variations to suit their particular necessities.

12. Experimentation and Learning Culture: Light-footed associations are encouraging a culture of trial and error, where it's protected to come up short and learn. This advances development and nonstop improvement.

13. Sustainability and Agile: A few associations are coordinating deft practices with manageability drives, utilising Spry's flexibility to help feasible practices and decrease ecological effects.

These developing patterns and practices mirror the continuous obligation to adaptability, cooperation, and client esteem, as associations endeavour to remain serious and responsive in the present unique business climate.

Conclusion

In the determination of a book like "Mastering Agile: A Comprehensive Guide to Agile Software Development," Jeffery M. Falgoust frequently wraps up the critically important points and experiences introduced through the book. Here is a synopsis of what you could track down in such an end:

1. Recap of Key Concepts: The decision ordinarily starts with a succinct recap of the essential deft ideas and systems examined in the book. This fills in as a sign of the centre rules that support light-footed programming improvement.

2. Emphasis on Dexterous Values: The creator repeats the four basic beliefs of the Coordinated Statement: people and cooperation, working programming, client joint effort, and answering change. The significance of these qualities in directing light-footed rehearsals is featured.

3. Iterative and Steady Development: The end highlights the meaning of iterative and gradual turn of events, a primary idea in Spry. It's underscored that continuous, little emphasis permits groups to adjust to changing necessities and convey esteem all the more now and again.

4. Continuous Improvement: The possibility of ceaseless improvement, frequently known as Kaizen, is a focal subject. Light-footed improvement isn't an objective but an excursion. Groups ought to continuously look for ways of upgrading their cycles and results.

5. Customer-Driven Approach: The book's decision emphasises the significance of a client-driven approach. Light-footed approaches are intended to adjust advancement endeavours to client requirements and inclinations.

6. Collaboration and Communication: Compelling coordinated effort and correspondence are featured as key achievement factors in light-footed. Cross-useful groups working intently together cultivate better comprehension and quicker critical thinking.

7. Adaptability and Flexibility: Lithe's versatility and adaptability are examined as fundamental characteristics. In a quickly changing business climate, lithe empowers associations to turn and answer new data and arising patterns.

8. Role of Leadership: The job of administration in supporting coordinated groups is highlighted. Coordinated pioneers are frequently viewed as worker pioneers who enable groups and eliminate impediments to their prosperity.

9. Scaling Agile: The end might address scaling deft practices for bigger associations. It could refer to systems like Protected, LeSS, and Nexus, which assist with broadening light-footed standards across numerous groups.

10. Challenges and Pitfalls: The creator recognizes normal difficulties and entanglements in taking on spry, for example, protection from change, absence of understanding, and the requirement for social movements. Defeating these difficulties is fundamental for a fruitful dexterous change.

11. Future Trends: The end might offer experiences into the future of Spry. It could examine arising patterns, like Spry's application in non-IT spaces, the joining of man-made intelligence and computerization, and the developing job of deft in a post-pandemic world.

12. Encouragement and Reflection: The end frequently urges perusers to proceed with their coordinated excursion and apply the standards and practices talked about in the book. It accentuates the significance of reflection and gaining for a fact.

In synopsis, the determination of a book on light-footed programming improvement ordinarily fills in as a last sign of the centre's standards, values, and practices of dexterity. It urges perusers to embrace these ideas, adjust them to their particular settings, and progress forward with their lithe excursion with an emphasis on conveying worth to clients and encouraging a culture of nonstop improvement.

www.ingramcontent.com/pod-product-compliance
Lightning Source LLC
Chambersburg PA
CBHW061010260726

48661CB00005B/2139